HANDBOOK OF ADAPTED PHYSICAL EDUCATION EQUIPMENT AND ITS USE

HANDBOOK OF ADAPTED PHYSICAL EDUCATION EQUIPMENT AND ITS USE

By
MICHAEL SOSNE, M.A.
Adapted Physical Education Teacher
Battle Creek Public Schools
Recreation Director
Southwestern Rehabilitation Center, Inc.
Battle Creek, Michigan

CHARLES C THOMAS • PUBLISHER
Springfield • Illinois • USA

Published and Distributed Throughout the World by

CHARLES C THOMAS • PUBLISHER
BANNERSTONE HOUSE
301-327 East Lawrence Avenue, Springfield, Illinois, U.S.A.

© *1973, by* CHARLES C THOMAS • PUBLISHER
ISBN 0-398-02782-X
Library of Congress Catalog Card Number: 72-11619

Printed in the United States of America

HH-11

To
THOMAS J. DE CARLO
*Teacher, coach and friend, who has
been a constant source of inspiration
throughout the years*

Handbook of Adapted Physical Education Equipment and
Its Use is geared to deal with the problems teachers have in
adapting physical education equipment to mentally and physically handicapped children. This book contains examples, suggestions and directions for adapting physical education equipment
to specific handicaps. Sources for physical education and adapted
physical education equipment and supplies are listed in the six
appendices.

The book is intended to be a useful reference to physical
education, special education and regular classroom teachers, attendant staff members of residential settings as well as members
of day training centers who are responsible for the education of
handicapped children. The material is presented in a concise,
informal manner. Included in this handbook are photographic
illustrations of adapted physical education equipment being used
by the handicapped.

The idea of this book is to assist inexperienced as well as
experienced teachers in planning for the handicapped in a program of physical education. Practical and useful pieces of adapted
physical education equipment are presented in the belief that
they will aid the teacher in adding to the total educational
experience of the student in his school life. These devices will
enable the child to be an active participant in leisure time activities that will carry over into adult life. The teacher and student
both will receive personal satisfaction through the use of specialized pieces of equipment.

This author truly believes that this book will inspire all
teachers to see that the mentally and physically handicapped do
have the necessary adapted devices available so that they, the
handicapped, will be able to say, "I can do it!"

MICHAEL SOSNE

ACKNOWLEDGMENTS

The author is truly indebted to Bruce L. Bachelder, Ph.D., Western Carolina Center, Morganton, North Carolina for taking and preparing a majority of the photographs appearing in this book. His expert photography has indeed been an invaluable addition to this book.

Acknowledgment must also go to my wife and children, who somehow put up with me through all this. To them I say "Thanks."

CONTENTS

HANDBOOK OF ADAPTED PHYSICAL EDUCATION EQUIPMENT AND ITS USE

IMPLICATIONS FOR PHYSICAL EDUCATION

Individuals with mental and physical handicaps will be found in regular classrooms, special education schools, residential settings and day training centers. It is extremely important for the teacher, recreational worker and attendant to recognize, understand and instruct a mentally and/or physically handicapped student. The instructor must be aware of special, and most time unique, needs of this student.

When the reader uses this handbook, he must realize that some of these students will exhibit one or more hanidcaps simultaneously. There will be instances where a student is not purely or solely a cerebral palsied individual. It is possible for the educable mentally retarded student to have visual and auditory problems along with his intellectual handicap. The person responsible for physical education in particular must know of the clinical and educational characteristics of his students.

This chapter will present each mental and physical handicap separately. It will discuss each condition as a separate entity as it relates to physical education. Each section is designed to inform the reader of what the implications for physical education are. The suggestions will aid the reader in planning an activity with predesigned goals, objectives, procedures and evaluations of individual performances. Description of the mental and physical handicaps will be mentioned as they relate to adapted physical education equipment.

Ideas for equipment and suggestions on how to use them in certain areas will be emphasized. The main points of this section are indivdual student programming in a physical education unit and special considerations in equipment. The student's vocational, social and family life are aspects that will be covered as they relate to equipmnt and the experience in the adapted program. Acquisition of skills during the physical activity are relevant to other areas of learning. Mainly, this section is designed to express what benefits the student can derive from having and using adapted physical education equipment as it affects the total person.

SLOW LEARNER

The slow learner will not need specialized pieces of adapted physical education equipment. He can best be educated in the regular classroom with slight adaptations to the program (Cruickshank and Johnson, 1967). This student will need what the normal child of his own age group needs in a comprehensive physical education program.

Color cues and the like would be beneficial and would allow the student to develop individual skills. His is more of a remedial need rather than a highly specialized one.

A precaution the instructor must take is to avoid frustrating situations. If this student is treated like other members of his peer group, but for slight changes, there will be no major problems. He will achieve success in his physical endeavors. The teacher can help in the child's communication development thorugh the use of planned group interaction. This student needs to become aware that he has something he can give to his classmates and to the activity as well.

EDUCABLE

Physical education for the educable mentally retarded individual is a very important segment of his total educational experience. This student needs to develop skills he can use in his leisure time, vocation and daily living. The physical education program must be suited to meet the immediate, future and distant future needs of each student in the program.

For the most part, the educable mentally retarded child is capable of learinng many physical activities. He must have a program presented to him in a clear, simple, but concise step-by-step manner. The introduction of adapted physical education equipment should be dealt with by utilizing the same step-by-step methodology. This student, as all students, should receive constant reinforcement of the activity through audiovisual materials and self-testing techniques. Graton (1964) mentions a well known fact that at times this student appears to be slow in his movements, unwilling to work, or disobedient, but actually his reaction to a direction is slower than that of the normal child.

Color-cuing certain parts of equipment is helpful, especially to the student who has difficulty in developing an awareness of left, right, top and bottom. Later, as the child learns these concepts, the teacher can introduce a non-color-cued piece of equipment. This procedure must be planned for well in advance of the end of the teaching unit. The teacher would benefit by having several pieces of equipment color-cued to varying degrees before he initiates a new unit. This method would be a timesaver for both student and teacher. Instructors would do best by saving some of the adapted devices used in former units.

Visual signs that the children see in their daily lives should be part of the physical education program. Such signs are STOP, ONE WAY, WALK, MEN, WOMEN, BUS STOP, NO PARKING, and many others. These signs can be used in conjunction with table games, floor games and obstacle course games. By using these signs in class, the student can become more aware of the meanings the signs hold and, hence, the physical education program is reinforcing and adding to the student's academic experience.

Geographical concepts can be dealt with in the same fashion. Children in the class can use large shapes to crawl through or over. These can be made from sheets of plywood with smooth, rounded edges. Geographical locations can be handled in the same manner. In an obstacle course, signs bearing words and phrases such as GO RIGHT, GO LEFT, GO UNDER, BOTTOM, TOP, CORNER, and more, could be placed at various stations to signify directions. All of the above concepts will add much to the well-rounded physical educational program.

Utilization of mathematical concepts is also possible. Target games can have interchangeable numerals on them to correspond to the academic level of the students playing the game. In a game like this, they would have to add several numbers together to get a score. Subtraction can be dealt with in a modified shuffleboard game. Many variations of this concept can be introduced by the teacher in traditional sport and recreational activities.

Equipment must be stimulating, desirable to use, and afford a challenge to the student on his own level of academic and physical accomplishments. Any piece of equipment should be of a particular make-up that allows this student to use it independently, without continuous assistance from the instructor. It should not be a complex device because this would defeat its sole purpose—that of being a piece of adapted physical education equipment. Many of these types of devices are presented and described in Chapter Four under the heading of a specific physical activity.

The adapted physical education equipment should also concern itself with the attainment of physical fitness, physical skills and establishment of a desire on the part of the student to initiate some self-directed physical activities. These might be a variety of community recreational activities, either school-related or at commercial recreational establishments.

TRAINABLE

The trainable mentally retarded student can learn basic elementary physical education skills. The programming and equipment must be kept simple. Clear and concise directions should be presented to this student. He must be familiarized with the equipment and its goals as the unit builds into a rewarding activity.

Immediate and long-range goals of physical skills should be established for each child in the physical education program. The trainable child can initially develop new physical skills to use in public or commercial recreational establishments. To develop these skills, he must be given ample time to learn how to use pieces of adapted physical education equipment and perfect his perceptual skills as well.

The level of instruction should be such that the child will be able to understand the simplest of directions and commands. Learning the names of the pieces of equipment will help the student develop his language skills and further facilitate the instruction of the unit. It is most important that the units of instruction have a large carry-over value to other areas of instruction. That is, one unit should be the basis for the next, and so on. This fact is not unique to the world of the retarded.

Adapted pieces of equipment should help develop basic large and small muscle skills. A percentage of these students have not perfected the skills of running, jumping, hopping or skipping. Therefore, the adapted devices must aid in the development of these and other motor skills.

Foot placement mats can be used to help direct the act of jumping or any of the above-mentioned skills. Outlines of a right and a left foot are drawn on a rubber or cloth material. The next set of footprints is one step in front of the first set. The student stands in the first set and, with assistance from the teacher, jumps to the second set. Teacher aid is recommended for the beginning trials until the child can accomplish the task by himself. Wooden slats, the width of the foot placement mat, and two inches high, can be used instead of foot tracings. This device is similar to a ladder, in that it has open spaces to step into. The student is asked to step, hop or jump over the boards to the next open section in front of him. A good progression is from the mat to the boards to no devices.

The reader should be aware that these students have motor-perceptual difficulties which make learning a difficult task. Repetition is needed with these pupils, along with reinforcement from all areas of instruction. Games of low organization, using gross motor movements and incorporation of language development, are to be stressed. It is best to keep to a few formations for games and drills. Different games can be played from circle, line and file formations. Even though the games are varied, the formations remain the same. This makes it easier for this student to participate in many types of games.

Pieces of adapted equipment can be interchanged from one activity to another. Implements used to scoop up balls or similar objects can also be used for striking balls, pushing blocks and more. The handles of these objects can be covered with varied types of materials that provide the student with a better grip. A somewhat coarse material that will not harm the student can be used for increased tactile awareness. Burlap, corduroy and Velcro® can be used, not only on handles, but on other surfaces that the student will have to hold on to for a better grip.

The emphasis here has been on developing physical and academic skills that will permit this student to be as independent as possible. These skills can lead to additional self-help skills which this indivdual needs very much.

As the student gets older and is still in a school-type setting, the physical education program should be geared to recreational activities. Throughout the years in the physical education program, this student should be acquiring skills that will be the basis for recreational activities. He certainly can be taught to bowl, roller skate and swim, to mention a few. These activities will have to be supervised by a qualified person when conducted on a group basis. A bowling league is a fine example of a supervised recreational activity.

The reader should develop a program for the trainable student that will compliment other areas of the student's instruction. All areas of instruction should work toward training this student in skills that will enable him to be an active part of his family and community.

INFIRM

The infirm individual is capable of participating in and gaining from the physical education program. The degree and extent of involvement in the program will of course depend on many factors. If the individual is confined to a bed for a majority of the time, then physical activities must be planned for the bedridden patient. This person can take part in group activities of various types. Through the use of adaptations to equipment and facilities, students can play musical instruments, badminton, balloon games, play ball games and use table games. The beds would have to be movable to allow for these individuals to become involved in the total program.

Those in wheelchairs who can move about independently can take part in many physical education activities. They can bowl, square dance, use table games, participate in specially designed small group activities and play miniature golf. If they cannot hold a bowling ball, for example, but can hold a shuffleboard stick or push a ball off a ramp, then they can bowl. The degree of participation by these people depends on the utilization of space, facilities and adapted equipment.

Those individuals who are able to use walkers to move about can take part in activities that require minimal physical action. A few examples of the types of activities in which the infirm person can be active are billiards, table tennis, bowling, horseshoes and active table games. Certain rules of the activity will have to be modified, but not to the extent that the original meaning of the game is lost.

This author has worked with infirm individuals where many of the preceding activities had to be conducted in the infirmary where these people lived. Hallways, wards, and spare rooms were used for severely involved individuals. These are by no means the ideal areas for physical education or recreation activities, but they did accomodate small numbers of residents who were unable to go to the gymnasium or activity field. At times additional staff members had to assist the physical education personnel in taking these people on field trips to a bowling establishment, roller skating rink or snow sledding. A highly structured program, including adapted equipment and, at times, numerous staff members, is needed to make this adapted program work.

AMYOTONIA CONGENITA

Students with this condition require a highly specialized physical education program. The program should be geared to utilizing the student's full range of physical abilities. Many students will require extensive numbers of adapted equipment items.

The size and weight of the special devices will be the main concern of the teacher. This student will need to have devices he can hold and manipulate by himself in a variety of units of instruction. For example, if the student is taking part in a badminton unit, the racquet should be lightweight with a short handle and a specially designed hand grip. The immediate goals for the special devices are ease and accuracy of movement.

Contact sports such as floor hockey, basketball and soccer

should not be entirely avoided. Specific rules and procedures should be adapted to meet the needs of this student. Special precautions should be taken in active games where bodily contact is likely to occur. This contact is of course on a limited basis with this student and should be well supervised. In a variety of activities hand guards, head protectors, safety goggles and safety belts should be used. Use of these safety devices will permit the student to enter the activity without the fear of being injured.

Ball games need not be played with the conventional playground balls. Smaller, partially deflated balls or beach balls could be used. Beach balls can be used in a volleyball unit with a degree of enjoyment and success for this student. When the beach ball is inflated to its fullest capacity, it becomes very easy to hit in the air. This student could serve the ball over a net that is lowered to an optimum height for him. With a change in the rules, he can serve the ball to a teammate who would then hit the ball over the net. This method has been used by this author with the understanding and cooperation of the other students in the class.

Balloons are other devices that could replace balls used with games now commonly played. Long balloons can be used in a modified football game and large, round ones can be used in a soccer game. They can also be used in a badminton game. Here, small balloons are inflated so they will not float in the air for a short time. If they are inflated too much, they will burst too soon. The balloons can be tied to a support overhead where two players can hit them back and forth to each other.

Hollow plastic practice balls are excellent for many activties. They are made in the size and shape of golf balls, softballs and footballs. This student can easily handle one because of its light weight. They can be used in a variety of floor and table games, where they can replace regulation balls used in many traditional sport activities.

Bowling can be a very enjoyable activity for this student. Special ramps will have to be constructed to initiate this activity for the student. This author has found this activity to be more enjoyable for the student when there is an adapted device present. One device, a bowling ramp, is designed so the student can aim and deliver the ball by himself. This method further aids in developing a stronger sense of independence in the student.

Floor and table games are excellent activities for this individual because of their versatility. They provide him with a wide variety of physical outlets he can take part in with his normal age peers in school or in the community. The games are adapted to him, but they are designed so anyone can play. Table games should be constructed with side and end boards. These boards will keep the playing materials on the board and not allow them to fall to the floor. Boundary lines can be made on the board where the action of the game will not take place. A shuffleboard game is an example in which the court is marked off on the board and the side boards help the student rebound his disk toward the target area.

Movement exploration with various pieces of equipment is a worthwhile activity for this student. This type of activity permits the student to explore the world of movement with some traditional and some specially designed devices. Hoops, wands of varied lengths and shapes, and thin ribbons of different colors can be used in a movement unit. These and many more devices can be used from the student's wheelchair, on the grass or on a mat. The variations the teacher can combine and use together are vast. All that is needed are the adapted devices that will allow the student to create his own movement patterns.

Wheelchair obstacle courses can be constructed, using a variety of turns, straight paths and slight inclines. In these courses, the student attempts to move his wheelchair through a sequence of obstacles, going from one type to another. The course he is on is preplanned so he will experience success. The obstacles should have signs on or around them instructing the student. As he approaches the end of the first obstacle, it can read TURN RIGHT or TURN LEFT. Different variations of this same idea can be used for each separate obstacle. Speed limit signs can also be used between obstacles, thus reinforcing mathematical concepts being taught in the classroom.

These are but a few of the adaptations to many activities the teacher can make for this individual in the physical education program. All of the activities sohuld have the interests of the student in mind. It is important to make the physical education program more meaningful to this student if we expect him to enjoy recreational activities.

BLIND AND PARTIALLY SIGHTED

The time to start the visually impaired child in the physical education program is when he is of preschool age. Under close supervision, this student can develop physical skills of varying degrees. The early school years will help this student form a better self-image and develop more confidence in himself. Only sound educational practices and procedures will bring this about.

Body awareness and spatial relationships are two important aspects of this student's educational programming. The young student should be able to develop these skills through successful encounters in large and small muscle activities. A technique used successfully by this author, when teaching gross motor activities, is to have the student place his hand on your arm as you move it in a certain task. This way the student can feel how the skill is performed. As the student practices the moves of a particular skill with the teacher, he can then attempt it by himself with an understanding of what is to be done. The teacher should also move the student's arms and legs to demonstrate the correct form used in various parts of a skill.

Balance or kinesthetic awareness is of vital importance in this student's training. Sighted persons receive visual cues to their surroundings and then respond accordingly. Visually impaired children do not have that benefit. They must rely on verbal cues given by the teacher, sense of touch and sounds emitted from the activity. Adapted auditory devices should be used in activities where direction is vital to the execution of the activity.

The most important responsibility the teacher has is to constantly respond to the physical efforts of the student. The response made by the teacher to the student is called feedback. The essentials of the activity will have to be described to him prior to and immediately after his physical endeavor has been made. Corrections should be made to the skill performance of the student to eliminate extra bodily movements or to further refine the skill.

Battery-operated buzzers and bells should be used to alert the student to a position, goal or target. It is necessary for the student to receive instructions on how to use these auditory aids. Sometimes the buzzer can be used as a warning device to alert the student to possibly dangerous portions of the playing area. As the student approaches the buzzer, he is aware that he has reached the boundary line of the field or court. The buzzer can warn of obstructions in the gymnasium. Such obstructions that sometimes cannot be moved are bleachers, room dividers or bars on the wall. It is best to plan for these hazards and have the activity going away from them. Too many buzzers will defeat the purpose of this device.

Bowling, basketball, archery, softball and floor hockey are but a few of the types of activities that require auditory aids. In basketball a battery-powered or plug-in type buzzer can be placed directly under that segment of the rim that attaches to the backboard. A plug-in device can be seen in Chapter Four. This way it can buzz and not be struck by the ball.

The buzzer can also be placed behind the center of an archery target. Thick sponge rubber should be placed between the back of the target and the buzzer. The target itself does afford protection to the buzzer, but this is an added precaution. The student positions himself in line with the target and aims for the sound where it is loudest. As he shoots his arrows, he receives feedback from the teacher as to where they have landed. This constantly helps him in improving his performance. The numbers on a clock can be used in reference to where his arrows have landed. When using more than one target, it is best to separate them so that the students do not become confused when trying to listen for their buzzer.

Engineers working for the Bell System of Western Electric have developed a ball the size of a softball that has a buzzer inside of it. It was developed so that the blind student could play softball. The student is instructed to swing when the sound is the loudest. The ball would then be in an optimum position for hitting. Again, immediate feedback is necessary to help the student adjust his swing and timing. The ball can also be placed on a batting T where he can swing at a stationary object. This will probably be the first step leading to the pitched ball. Balls thrown or hit on the ground can be approached by the use of this built-in buzzer. The student can locate the ball by listening for the buzzing sound. When he finds it, he can throw it to a partner who is nearby. His partner can indicate where he is by calling out to him.

A buzzer is extremely valuable in bowling. It should be used to direct the student to the strike zone in the pins. The teacher should construct a durable backstop that will withstand being hit by heavy balls and pins. A backstop made of thick cushions or a number of tumbling mats piled one on the other is fine for classroom use. The mats should be set in a semicircle formation. This way they stay in the area when struck by the ball. Place the buzzer on a board above the backstop at the desired spot you wish the student to aim toward. Each time he bowls, different pins will remain standing. It is wise to have four hooks on the board to represent the area where the pins are standing. You should be constantly giving the student feedback about his performance. Saying to him that he knocked all the pins over is not good enough. Tell him how close he came to the buzzer and where he hit the pins. As his skill increases, you can lengthen the distance from which he bowls. Every time the distance is increased, the student will have to readjust his perception of the auditory aid. After a while, he will no longer need the use of the buzzer, but will rely on the skills he developed in this activity. He should bowl from one consistent place on the lane. This will give him a constant point of reference on all commercial bowling lanes. The natural sequence of instructional skills should be working toward this goal.

Bells similar to those used in infant toys can be used in various ball activities. A ball with bells in it can be used in a modified hockey game. The ball is slightly deflated so that it will not roll away each time it is hit. A ball the size of a softball would be suitable for this purpose. Another type of ball that would allow students to have a good target is a small beach ball. Bells can also be used in a hollow plastic hockey puck. The teacher can make his own pucks from a variety of empty plastic containers used in the home. Small plastic bowls, with lids, are best for this purpose. Make sure that the lid is securely fastened to the bowl. Any number of bells can be placed in the bowl for added sound. This device is light enough to use without rolling away from the student. It was this author's experience that the plastic food container held up for a long time before having to be replaced.

Goal nets are used in hockey, soccer and other activities that require the student to hit an object into a goal. Buzzers should be placed at each goal behind the net. The student who is the goalkeeper should be instructed in how to block the puck or ball. He should have all of the proper safety equipment regardless of prior instructions or his skill as a goalkeeper. It is the teacher's responsibility to decide when a blind or partially sighted student should take this position.

A partially deflated ball or large plastic bottle can be used indoors or out for a soccer game. Firm bottles are best for this purpose. When playing soccer inside, empty plastic bottles can be placed around the perimeter of the playing area. As the student comes in contact with one, he knows he is at the side line. The risk of injury to the student is diminished by using these bottles. Laundry departments of most large schools and residential settings will use many of these bottles during the course of a year. They can be saved for not only soccer, but for a variety of other uses that will be mentioned throughout this book.

When conducting a soccer game out-of-doors, the bottles should be placed on the side lines and filled with water. Transporting them to and from the field empty will make them easier to carry. Once out there, the teacher could fill them half way so they will stay in place.

Track and field events can be conducted with some adaptations to equipment. Straight running will be used for sprint and long distance events. A continuous nylon rope secured to a pole at the starting and finish line will guide the runner. The rope should be three feet from the ground. The student runs along side of the guide rope holding a short rope that is attached to a round metal ring which slides freely over the guide rope. The rope should go past the finish line. A round disk should be placed on the guide rope to signal to the runner when he has reached the finish line. For safety, there should be at least two inches of foam rubber on the disk to prevent injury to his hand. When he reaches the disk it will slide, thereby signaling him to slow down. There should be at least six more feet of the guide rope after the disk at the finish line. This will allow the student enough time to slow down safely. A track could be set up to accomodate three or four runners.

Field events, such as shot put and discus, can be changed slightly. The portable buzzer mentioned previously could be used here with much positive effect. The student would get set in the throwing position and aim for the sound.

Table games such as table tennis, nok hockey and other recreational games are valuable activities for this student to develop for his total physical education program. In table tennis, a plastic practice ball can be secured to one end of a string with the other end connected to the racquet handle. Placing a bell inside the ball will add to the auditory assistance of the device. The length of the string should be from the student to approximately two feet over the net. As the student develops a smooth stroke, the use of another device is called for. A short pole attached to the side of the table, next to the net, has a ball and string attached to it. There is a sponge rubber ball at the end of the string. Any size ball can be used in this game. Two players can use this device without having to retrieve the ball every time one of them misses it.

A nok hockey set can be modified slightly by making larger holes for the puck to go through and having a bell set in the hole to signal a score. There should also be small cloth bags at either goal to catch the puck. The center spot, which is used to start a game, should have a slight, round indentation. In this way, this student can start a game by himself.

Floor games such as horseshoes, shuffleboard and floor tennis can also be adapted for this student. In horseshoes, a buzzer can be placed inside a wooden box. A short pole is attached to the top of the box above the buzzer. The buzzer will have to be secured to the bottom of the box by two wide rubber elastic bands. Strips from a tire inner tube would be excellent for this purpose. Before playing the game, the student would need to feel how high the pole is off the floor and how far it is from him. Distances can be changed as the proficiency of the individual student increases.

Shuffleboard can be adapted by placing this same wooden box at the end of the court. The buzzer will be behind the section that says TEN OFF. Two short standards can be placed behind the width of the court. A strip of rubber from a tire inner tube is attached to and connects each standard. As the pucks hit the rubber strip, they will rebound back to the court. The tighter the strip, the further the pucks will rebound. The standards are made from old coffee cans filled partially with cement. Many types of standards can be made this way to suit a vast variety of activities. Masking tape can be used to outline the numbered areas used for scoring. Another method that can be used is that of cutting numerals from fine-grained sandpaper and placing them in the scoring areas. The boundary lines of the scoring area can be outlined in this same way. The tops of one player's pucks can be covered with this same material.

Two students can play floor tennis at one time. The students stand at opposite ends of the court, facing one another. The horizontal line in the middle of the court represents the net. There is a string here, four inches from the ground, with three or four bells on it, going from one side of the court to the other. A ball attached to a tetherball standard is placed at midcourt along the sidelines. One student bounces the ball to the other, trying not to hit the string. If he does, the bells ring and the students know a point has been scored. The students cannot lose the ball because it is attached to the standard. Any size court can be made from an old sheet or whatever the teacher has at hand.

Folk, square and social dancing are very important socialization experiences for this student. His own positive self-image will be enhanced by knowing that he can take part in an activity his sighted peers do. There will be a need for individualized instructions and procedures in this unit. The use of various dance formations will facilitate a more successful unit. Keeping the directions simple and easy to follow will also have a positive influence on the students. The speed of the music will also have some bearing on the dance unit as a whole. As the students develop basic dance steps, they will ask for faster music.

A trained swimming instructor will need to be present when the visually handicapped student is learning how to swim. Developing confidence in himself and the instructor is of great importance. The student will find it to his advantage to familiarize himself with the pool surroundings before the actual swimming takes place. He will need to know where each ladder is located, in the shallow and in the deep ends. Constant checks on the progress of the student are necessary. The student should also be constantly receiving feedback. Arm movements in many strokes will have to be executed with the direct help of the instructor. Direct physical contact by the teacher is required in this activity, in order for the student to feel the correct sequence of movements in a desired swimming skill.

Removable eyelets can be placed on the outer edges of the swimming pool. These will be for the guide ropes that stretch the width of the pool. The student can swim the width, going a shorter distance in a safer area. This way, more swimmers can be practicing at one time than if they were to go the length of the pool. As each student's swimming ability increases, he could move one lane at a time toward the deep end of the pool. A low-pitched, portable buzzer should be used at pool-side to aid the students in swimming straight. The device should be protected from moisture as much as possible. The sound should also be able to be heard under water.

Gymnastics is an excellent activity for the visually impaired student to help him develop better coordination of his limbs. Some of the equipment in this activity remains stationary. This will help him greatly because he will only have to manipulate his own body on each piece of equipment. Adequate spotting and safety precautions will have to be taken in all events in the gymnastics unit. Work on the trampoline will be exciting for this student if the following safety rules are observed.

There should always be at least four competent spotters around the trampoline. When the student is prepared to go on the trampoline for the first time, he will have to wear an overhead spotting belt. The belt is placed around the student's waist. Two ropes, one on each side of the belt, go up to the ceiling through two separate pulleys. These pulleys are about fifteen feet apart over the trampoline. The ropes come down to the floor and are controlled by the teacher standing next to the trampoline. This way, the teacher has complete control over the movements of the student. This will give the student a full sense of confidence that he will not be injured. As he progresses, the belt can be removed for those stunts he has successfully accomplished in the belt.

Rope climbing can be conducted in this same safe manner. As the student climbs up the rope, the teacher is pulling on the spotting belt ropes. Climbing only part of the way up the rope is recommended for the beginner. As he develops greater ability and strength, he can go to the top without the belt.

Tumbling can be executed with no special equipment or procedures. In this event, the blind or partially sighted student will follow the same safety rules and regulations as the sighted student. The physical contact method between the student and teacher will be utilized here for the purpose of teaching the student how to perform various tumbling stunts.

There are many more sport and recreational activities this student can participate in if given appropriate equipment and individualized instructions. The reader should use the statements and suggestions made in this section as a guide for planning for the visually handicapped student in a recreation or physical education program.

CARDIAC CONDITIONS

Before starting a program of physical education for the student with a cardiac condition, the teacher should have a written permission or release form from the student's physician. The form should state what activities the student can take part in. The physician will give his approval for full, partial, limited or minimal participation, with various restrictions. This is a safe course of action on the part of the teacher to protect the health and safety of the student, and to protect his own position. When the permission form has been received by the teacher, he will then know what he can do with and for the student with a known cardiac condition. A physical activity form can be seen in Chapter Five.

The reader must first relate the equipment to the specific activity when initially programming for this student. If the individual's condition is severe, he will then need to participate in a wide variety of table games and mild adaptations of individual sports. The equipment must not confine the student, but allow him to be active. Each device should facilitate ease of motion and not tire the student.

Any student with a cardiac condition should be made to realistically look at his condition in respect to physical education and what he can hope to obtain from the class. This individual will be limited in this type of educational program, but he should know that there are various units of instruction he can take part in and realize success. This can be through the use of expert supervision, planning and adapted physical education equipment.

During the course of his education, he must be aware of his limitations in such activities as climbing, running, jumping, weight resistive exercises and combatives. Being aware of these limitations will help the student to establish himself in the program. If, for example, he is given a lower obstacle to climb rather than none at all, he will be involved. This same idea applies to equipment he can use by himself. A lighter weight tennis or badminton racquet will allow the student to continue in the game for a longer period without becoming too fatigued.

Frequent rest periods should be planned for this student by the physical education teacher. The frequency and duration of the rest periods should be directed by the student's physician. Different activities require varied schedules of rest. Some activities will not require any rest periods, thereby permitting the student a full class period. If and when the student's condition improves, the number of rest periods and their duration can be lessened.

This, too, is a decision to be made by the physician. This author believes that the physical education teacher should make objective reports to the physician concerning the over-all progress of the student. Some restrictions may be changed one way or another.

Contact between the teacher and physician is vital when the student's health and education are at stake.

Keeping the program as normal as possible for this student is very important. Some students cannot see where there is a difference between themselves and their normal peers. Their feelings of self-confidence must be increased by the methods described in this section.

CEREBRAL PALSY

It is not the role of the adapted physical education program to emphasize perfection of physical skills, but to aid the student in developing greater control of his muscular actions in recreational activities. In time, the student will be able to perform skills that require deliberate movements by first learning how to relax during the execution of the skill. Not all students will develop this skill or have complete voluntary muscular control, but the intent of the adapted equipment is to aid the student in skills he finds difficult. This author has found that a particular set of pre-established instructions works best. The instructions are given to the student prior to each new skill or game. They direct the student to first recall the steps of the particular skill, relax, perform the skill, and immediately relax again. This technique has been successful for the student with a more than moderate degree of physical involvement.

On one occasion, this author had the opportunity to work with a student who had a severe case of athetoid cerebral palsy. He was taking part in the bowling unit his class was beginning. Various types of adapted pieces of equipment were tried so that he could bowl. Boards, ramps and push devices were presented to him with little success. Finally, he attempted to bowl while out of his wheelchair. He bowled on his hands and knees from the foul line of a regulation lane. This student was able to bowl at this facility only after hours of practice at his own school. His right forearm was positioned on the floor in front of his knees. A rectangular piece of plywood was made into a shield with three Velcro straps that went around his forearm. The striking surface was covered with foam rubber so that the ball would not slide off the board. The ball was placed against his forearm so that when he pushed his forearm forward, the ball would roll toward the pins. The above-mentioned relaxation method was used with this boy. His own personal desire to bowl by himself prompted this mode of bowling. Using this procedure and device, he was able to knock some pins down. During one game he earned a strike and a spare.

The student with a severe condition of the ataxic type of cerebral palsy may not be able to perform various activities skillfully that call for kinesthetic or balance skills. It would be difficult for him to participate in games where he has to run and kick a ball as in soccer, run and hit a puck as in hockey, or catch a moving ball as in softball. He will be able to experience success in games such as those mentioned above, if he can position himself in one general area where the ball would come to him and give him ample time to react.

Swimming is an excellent activity for all types of cerebral palsy conditions. The bouyancy offered by the water is an atmosphere which is conducive to freer and more relaxed movements of his limbs. The use of adapted swimming devices will help the student in his efforts toward semi-independent or independent swimming. This swimming device can be seen in Chapter Four with additional discussion. The teacher can use many variations of these swimming devices to reach the above-mentioned goals of swimming ability.

The athetoid cerebral palsied student will be able to move at a slower pace in the water and still remain afloat with the use of these aids. As he develops a degree of proficiency with the swimming aids, he can concentrate on the steps of the stroke he is learning and not concern himself about remaining afloat. This way, the teacher is not developing a false sense of reliance on the devices on the part of the student, but rather he is developing skills needed for swimming. The same technique would be employed for other types of this condition.

Folk, square and social dancing are suitable activities for all types and degrees of cerebral palsy conditions. The dance formations can be varied to accommodate each individual student. Two lines of students facing each other is one formation used successfully by this author. The students are side-by-side and about three feet away from each other. Their partners are across from them and about four feet away.

At the beginning of a folk or square dance unit, it is best to use a slower tempo record without recorded directions. The teacher should always make up a set of directions in advance, suited to a particular group of students. This can be done on a cassette tape recorder or standard reel type. The directions or calls on the tape should be those maneuvers that the class has successfully completed. As new maneuvers are added to the dance, new tapes should be made. By the time the teacher uses all of the tapes for the unit, he will have an excellent progression of skills used for physically handicapped children.

Markers could be used to signify the first and last positions on the dance line. The markers could be wide pieces of tape with numbers on them or color-cued patches, such as green for the first position and red for the last. Arrows pointing the direction the dancers are to go could also be placed on the floor, at the beginning of each new dance, or for each new maneuver in a dance.

Social dancing will have to be geared to the age of the students. This type of unit has had most success in conjunction with the folk and square dance units. The teacher can group the students into junior high and high school ages for dance instruction and interest levels.

Many table games can be adapted to the cerebral palsied student. If he is in a wheelchair, then the table he is playing at would have to be adapted to his seated height. Arm length must also be taken into account for certain types of games. Nok hockey games could be on a turntable where the students do not have to move themselves to the other side of the table. All they do is turn the game to a position where they can hit the puck. Games where the student has to retrieve his own playing devices should be small enough to allow him to be independent in the execution of the game. Most games can be enjoyed by this student if they are the right size. It would be best if the game could be transported by the student, without help, to and from the games storage site. This will build a sense of responsibility in the student.

Table tennis is another game that does not have to kept at the regulation size for this student. The length and width can be modified along with the height of the table. A larger two-handled racquet can be used to aid the student in meeting the ball more easily. Sides can be built onto the table to prevent the ball from getting away from the players who are in wheelchairs or on crutches. These students can also use a pole next to the table that has the ball attached to it by a string. This way neither of them would have to chase the ball if it were to go over the boards.

Target games can be constructed so that the cerebral palsied student will be able to hit a desired area or object. The spaces or numbered areas should be clearly marked and large enough so he has a good chance of scoring.

The teacher could build an easy to use billiard table. A thin plywood sheet, covered with a smooth cloth material, is needed for the table surface. The most important device for this game is the semi-stationary pool cue. The teacher should drill holes at varying intervals on the top of the side and end boards. An eyelet will fit down into these holes. The pool cue will then fit into the hole in the eyelet and the student can play the game without becoming too frustrated. He will be able to keep the stick straight and level when shooting. The stick itself can be made from different sizes of wooden dowels with rubber tips placed on the ends. Adhesive tape placed on the handle would afford the student a better surface to grip than would the plain stick itself. Various sizes of rubber tips can be found in most variety stores.

Floor games for this student can consist of horseshoes, shuffleboard, miniature golf and modified table games played on the floor. Each of these activities can be adapted to the special needs of each student. The upright that the student aims for in a game of horseshoes, should be placed on a rubber or carpet mat to protect the gymnasium floor. A mat will also help keep the horseshoes close to the upright. The student who is in a wheelchair might find it difficult to retrieve the horseshoes from the floor. A hole can be made in the horseshoe, so the student can pick it up by using a wooden dowel that fits firmly into the hole. This device will make the student that much more independent. This procedure has been used by this author with cerebral palsied students with much success.

Tumbling mats can be placed around the shuffleboard court to aid the students in keeping the pucks on the playing area. Thicker shuffleboard pucks will present a larger target for the student to push. The student will be better able to keep the stick behind the larger sized puck. A hole can be made in the puck if it proves to be too heavy for a particular student. This way it changes the weight, but not the size of the puck. Soft wood is best for this purpose. The puck can be painted in any number of ways, but the bottom should not be. It should be smooth and waxed so that it will slide more easily.

A narrow, smooth wooden ramp can be used for horseshoes and shuffleboard for severely involved students. Side boards should be placed on the ramp to keep the puck from falling off before it reaches the bottom. The ramp can be placed between the student's legs, if possible, or to one side of him on the seat of his wheelchair. The puck is placed so that it is partially on the student's lap and partially on the edge of the ramp. In this way, the student is the one who pushes the puck down the ramp by himself.

Other floor games can be played with balls of various sizes and weights. A slightly deflated ball can be used so that the student will have better control in holding and throwing it. Strings can be attached to some balls for use in a group setting where many of the pupils are severely involved. The ball will still have freedom of movement, but it will also stay close to the students where they can retrieve it very easily.

Floor hockey can be played in a variety of ways. The student who is on crutches can have the blade of an old hockey stick secured to the end of one of his crutches. This way, he does not have to hold on to an additional item. If he did not have the blade secured to the bottom of the crutch, he would have to stop, support himself on his arm rests, which is undesirable, and then play from an awkward position. A hollow pastic hockey puck would work very well for some students, but others would need a bigger device. One device that has proven to be a valuable replacement is a firm, slant-sided, empty plastic food container— preferably one with the lid attached. This container can be struck very hard and the lid will stay on. It will slide on a gymnasium floor freely, but it will not roll away from the student so that he has to spend much of his time chasing it. This container also works well on a grass field. Its size will allow the student who is in a wheelchair or on crutches to hit it easily, without getting the blade of the hockey stick caught in the grass.

Volleyball can be played with a beach ball instead of a regulation ball. Because the beach ball is much lighter, it stays in the air longer and will give the student more time to prepare himself to hit it over the net. It is also a larger target, which aids the student who has difficulty in striking a small object. For practice, a beach ball can be placed on a tetherball standard. This way, the student can practice his volleyball skills and not have to chase after the ball each time he hits it away from his area.

Balloons can also be used in a volleyball game. They afford the student that much more time to return the balloon over the net or to his partner. Large balloons would be better than small ones from the standpoint of size of the target.

Where possible, several nets set at different heights should be used. Those students who are seated in wheelchairs may need a net set at one height, whereas those students who are on crutches and without aids can use a net set higher, and one group of students will use a net set close to the regulation height. Various students who are in wheelchairs will be able to function quite well from the second highest or highest net.

Basketball can be adapted to students with cerebral palsy by simply lowering the basket. A photograph of this device can be seen in Chapter Four, along with additional discussion. A formula this author has used to determine the height of the basket is to add three feet above the head of the tallest student seated in a wheelchair. This applies only to a group of students who are all in wheelchairs and not a mixture of students on crutches, in wheelchairs or without ambulation aids. Two, and possibly three, portable backboards should be used in one class, one basket being used for each group mentioned above. If the teacher does not have enough students in his class to make three groups of sufficient size, then he will have to modify the rules of the game.

One way to accomodate a class of students who are operating from the three different modes of movement is to have period assignments. In the first period, all of the ambulatory students are assigned to shoot the ball at the basket. The other students are to dribble and pass the ball. In the next period, the students who are in wheelchairs are the shooters while the students who are on crutches and those without aids dribble and pass the ball. For the last period, the students on crutches are the shooters. As each shooting group changes, so does the height of the basket.

The school's maintenance shop can make a basketball rim that is larger than the regulation type. It would be a good idea to have three sizes of rims in use for the students who need a larger target. These rims should be made so that they can be easily taken off and replaced for different groups in the same class.

Basketballs are made in two regulation sizes. One size is used in regular high school physical education classes and the other is used at the elementary and junior high school levels. The difference in sizes is noticeable when they are compared with each other. When using either one, this author recommends the rubber-covered ball because the student will have a better grasp on the ball. Playground balls can also be used for this activity. These balls come in a variety of sizes. Here, too, a beach ball can be used during a class session.

Badminton is an additional activity that can be adapted to the student with cerebral palsy. A special glove can be used by the student who has difficulty in grasping the handle of the racquet. The hook side of Velcro is sewn to the palm of the glove and the tape side is glued and nailed to the handle of the racquet. This will afford the student a more secure grip of the racquet. A lightweight, short-handled racquet can also be used by this student.

The height of the net can be modified to the three groups of students mentioned previously in this section. A string can be tied to both of the standards to which the net is secured. Several metal rings that slide freely are on the string. Attached to each ring is a short string with a plastic practice ball or badminton birdie. At the beginning of the lesson, each student can practice hitting one of these objects. As the student hits the ball or birdie, the metal ring turns around on the string. This way, the student always has the birdie within his reach, even though he might hit it a few feet away from himself.

The above mentioned activities and suggestions are a beginning for more individualized adaptations of physical education and recreation activities. The simplest and most efficient methods have been presented to the reader to involve the handicapped child in the adapted physical education program.

DEAF AND HARD-OF-HEARING

Much of the physical education program for the deaf and hard-of-hearing students revolves around physical demonstration

as a form of explanation by the teacher. Explanation, demonstration and then the incorporation of the two is utilized to instruct these pupils. The child who is deaf will have difficulty in any one of these phases of instruction if he does not clearly understand the instructions or the instructor. Many repetitions of the same instruction will have to be given to some students before they will be able to carry out the instructions. These steps need to be taken to insure the best possible comprehension of the activity by the student. This author has found in his work with the hearing-impaired student that it is advantageous to have eye contact with the student when describing an activity or giving instructions. If he can lip-read the teacher and understand any physical gestures he makes, the student will stand a better chance of comprehending the activity.

There should be a structured set of pre-established commands that signify procedures on the gymnasium floor, the playground, and especially in the swimming pool. Not all of the deaf children will hear the teacher's whistle. When the class is in the gymnasium the teacher can use his whistle and then place his hand in the air above his head. When a hearing student notices the sound, he can place his hand above his head to signal to a nonhearing student that the activity must come to halt. The hearing-impaired individual will then know he has to stop and wait for the next direction.

The equipment for the deaf and hard-of-hearing student does not need to be of a highly specialized nature. Regular pieces of equipment can be used by these students in their physical education program. It is the programming that needs to be adapted to these students in the form of special safety precautions and instructional procedures.

The physical education equipment should be explained to the student in terms of how it is to be used. This is a step-by-step procedure. After the student acquires skill in the use of the equipment, he will also develop a sense of positive independence, responsibility and self-confidence when it comes time to perform other related skills.

For the most part, the student who is hard-of-hearing is able to function very well in the regular physical education class. He would need to be close to the instructor in order to more accurately hear and understand the directions. If he wears a hearing aid, he would of course be expected to follow the safety rules set down by the instructor for various activities.

Both the deaf and hard of hearing students should take part in as many physical activities as they can. This would include integration with the hearing students. It is this author's belief that both verbal and physical explanations for giving instructions should be used equally. This author has found that the hearing-impaired student retains the rules of a game, names of objects he uses and the types of formations used, for a longer period of time when he attempts to say them. This type of programming can only come about with a close working relationship with the student's classroom teacher and the physical education teacher. In no way does this author mean to imply that a deaf student, who cannot speak, will be talking in the physical education class, but rather he will be better able to associate the names of articles, rules and procedures to varied activities when the need arises. In this way, the physical education teacher is aiding in the student's language development. These skills will certainly make him a more active participant in community recreational activities.

EPILEPSY

Physical education should be a significant part of this student's educational program. Because of drug therapy, many students are now in special education schools, classes for exceptional children in regular grade schools and in day-training centers. Years ago, these students were cared for in residential settings because of their medical problem. The student who must reside in a residential setting today is indeed a severe case. The use of drugs to control seizures has done much to bring these people into the normal flow of society.

Special devices or adaptations to equipment are not necessarily vital aspects of the physical education program for this individual. If he also has some other handicap, he will be discussed in one of the other sections of this chapter. The student with this condition is presented for discussion because of special considerations that need to be made in the programming of certain physical education and recreational activities.

Vigorous physical activity, combined with an adequate diet and ample rest, tends to diminish the number of seizures the student has. On the other hand, limiting the degree and type of activity the student takes part in may tend to bring on more seizures.

Activities that present a degree of risk should be avoided. This does not mean that the entire scope of the sport or recreational activity need be eliminated from the student's experience. All possible areas of the activity should be viewed by the physical education teacher, physician and parents for segments that the student can participate in with a large margin of personal safety.

One activity which does present a degree of risk, but one that many students find enjoyable, is gymnastics. Tumbling, horizontal bar, still rings and trampoline are but a few of the events in this sport that this student can enjoy with the proper training. With adequate spotting and safety procedures, this student may participate in almost all of the gymnastic events, with the exception of rope climbing. This specific activity should be eliminated because the student may have a seizure or become unconscious when he is at the top of the rope. This rule would apply to the student who is currently having seizures.

Swimming is an activity in which he can be involved while following certain precautions. When it is a school-directed program, a competent instructor or lifeguard should be aware of the student's condition. During recreational swimming sessions, this student should swim with a reliable companion who is also aware of his condition.

Bicycle riding can be a delight for this student by employing certain safeguards. Riding in heavy traffic should be discouraged. If he is going to ride in an area where there is heavy traffic, he should have a companion along with him.

Contact sports are not to be totally avoided. For example, football, wrestling, soccer and floor hockey can be played by this student. Livingston (1963) cites examples of his patients involved in body contact sports. Careful planning should take place before the student is involved in a new activity to avoid undue fatigue or injuries.

The main goal of the adapted physical education program for this student is to develop his emotional and social interactions through the use of individualized instruction. The accomplishment of varied physical skills will aid in the development of his total positive self-image.

HYDROCEPHALUS

The hydrocephalic individual may also suffer from other physical handicaps. This section is devoted to the indivdual who has a moderate or severe condition.

The student with the moderate condition can oftentimes be found in a public or special education school in his own community. Adaptations in programming should be made for the moderately involved individual. Special devices will not necessarily be required. An occasion might arise where the student's physician requests that he wear a specially designed safety helmet for a particular activity, but this would be a special instance.

A refined sense of balance and spatial awareness are two areas the moderately involved individual will have to develop. These and other perceptual skills should be covered in the course of his instruction. Movement education, gymnastics and swimming are excellent activities for this student. In these activities, he can improve his kinesthetic sense which is the basis for many other activities.

The more severely involved individual will need specially designed equipment. If he uses a wheelchair, then he will need a specially constructed headrest. The physical education teacher should help in designing the headrest because the student will need to have adequate support and protection in physical education activities.

Rules, procedures and techniques will have to be adapted in order for the student to participate. He will require lighter weight and possibly larger pieces of equipment. The larger device does not mean that it has to be heavier. The reason for the increased size of some devices is because this student does not have the physical freedom of head movement. He would need a larger striking device for softball, badminton, miniature golf, floor hockey and horseshoes, to mention a few.

The severly involved student will also exhibit vision and auditory problems stemming from his initial condition. Mental retardation is another characteristic of the severely involved hydrocephalic individual. All of the preceding characteristics can be present to varying degrees.

There are two optimum positions that the severely handicapped student will assume for participation in physical education and recreational activities. These are lying on his back or on either side. He will probably be using a contoured headrest of some type. This type of situation must be considered in the programming of this student.

Floor games are excellent for this student. Horseshoes can be made of hollow plastic and the horseshoe pin can be a used paper towel roll. With the pin this size, the student is assured of hitting it frequently. Small bean bags should be used with a large target. This way the student can hold the bean bag by himself and also be able to throw it through a hole in the target. Many variations of targets can be used by this student. Another game can be played where the student has to push foam rubber shapes through holes in a box. The holes are color-coordinated with the foam rubber shapes. After he pushes the shapes through the holes, he has to take them out of the back of the box.

A tripod can be set up over the student with a large, empty plastic bottle hanging at the end of a string. The student is equipped with a suitable striking object. Bells ring inside the bottle as the student hits it. Many variations of this game can be made with various materials. Whatever the object is, it should be bright and stimulating to the student. He does not have to hit it with an implement of some kind, he could use his own hands. Another example of objects to be placed on the tripod would be foam rubber animal shapes with brightly painted bells on them.

Other active games can be adapted to this student. Push games, using balls or blocks, can be played. Bowling, hockey and shuffleboard-type games can be added to this student's realm of physical experiences. The student can push a large ball into a group of plastic bottles made up to look like clowns, animals or some other children's toys. Painted faces with funny-looking ears could be added to the bottles.

A nok hockey-type board can be made where the student has to push a block into a hole using a stick. The stick is curved so that it will hold the block against it, allowing the student to push it into the hole. A miniature obstacle course could be made on the board. It can consist of two blocks set in front of the hole, but with enough room for the student's block to go through. The teacher can utilize many varied pieces of equipment for games of this type.

One way to increase the physical involvement of this student is to have him help in the construction of the equipment. Pasting, cutting and painting are skills this student may be able to do or learn. As long as the student is able to hold a brush, he can help. He can certainly help paint the plastic bottles, using water colors. The faces that go on the bottles can be pasted on by this student. The physical education teacher must adapt all aspects of the program to the student and his environment.

Magnetic game boards can be used with those students who have to remain on their backs or sides for much of the time. Many variety stores carry magnets of all shapes and sizes. Large hot plates are best for the game board. A frame with four adjustable legs should be used to hold the board. This way the frame can be tilted to the child's lying position. The edges of the game board rest on the inside ledge of the frame. The student can play by raising his hands up to the board. He can move the magnets on the board in an easy manner. The same frame can serve for many different games.

Ramp games can be constructed for the student who can be in a reclining position. The ramp has side boards on it so the moving objects will remain on the playing area. A modified bowling game can be played by this student. The student pushes a disk down the ramp to one of the plastic bottles at the end of the ramp. These are small bottles set in a large box. The same procedure can be used for shuffleboard and miniature golf-type games.

Another variation of the ramp game the student can play is where he has to push a ball into a billiard-type board. There are side boards on this game that will keep the ball from going off. A bell system can be placed in each hole on the board. The bells can be suspended from rubber bands. When the bell rings it tells the player the ball went through the hole. This system will work with the student who still has a functional degree of auditory perception.

This student should be encouraged to use his feet to take part in physical activities. He can participate in a circle game with other students where the object is to kick the ball to each other. This is a good game for students of limited physical movement in their upper limbs or who cannot sit up. A plastic beach ball is excellent for this activity. By using his feet, he can also take part in rhythmical activities. Musical instruments can be used in such activities. With a drumstick secured to the student's foot, he can enjoy the thrill of playing an instrument that will make music. A special footrest might have to be made, but this is expected. Other students can be playing other instruments to make their own song. This is an excellent opportunity to have social interaction that these children need. The music the students make can be recorded on a tape recorder and played back to them after they are through. They will receive much enjoyment from this.

The goal of the adapted physical education program for this student is to present activities to him that he will enjoy participating in by himself, or with another child. The games and activities should stimulate the student's perceptual areas. If the student is only capable of using his arms to a limited degree and has minimal vision, then these areas should not be emphasized in the types of games he plays. He should be planned and programmed for in terms of his present physical and mental abilities.

MICROCEPHALUS

This student should have adaptations in his program as they relate to physical skill achievement, language development and development of additional preceptual skill areas. The microcephalic student will need most of the same physical and academic considerations in the physical education program as the educable and trainable mentally retarded individual. In some instances, he will require a program of recreational activities similar to that of the infirm individual.

Perceptual skill development should be in the areas of auditory discrimination, figure-ground perception, tactile discrimination and form recognition. These are areas that need to be developed for the student's successful training in recreational skills and self-help skills.

Table and floor games can consist of a few objects in each and be in one, two or three colors. A square box can be constructed in which there are four compartments. In each section there is a painted geometric shape. The top right-hand corner could be a red square, the top left-hand corner a green circle, and so on. The background should be painted white to show contrast. The student has four sponges corresponding to the colors and shapes of the forms in the box. The sponges can be colored by using fabric dye. Other games of low organization used by the educable and trainable mentally retarded student can be used by this individual.

Bicycle riding is an excellent activity for this student, because it will develop reciprocal motion in the lower limbs. This physical action is vital to help the student develop his walking, running and jumping skills. The elementary school years, or initial school years, should be the period when this student is taught how to ride a three-wheeled bicycle. Too many times this type of physical activity is conducted on a recreational basis. The place for this teaching activity is in the adapted physical education program. There are three-wheeled bikes that are not chain-driven and these are the familiar tricycles we see young children riding. There are also three-wheeled bicycles that are chain driven and are much larger than the conventional tricycle. Special adaptations can be made for the student who has difficulty holding his feet on the pedals. A simple Velcro strap can be secured to the inside and outside edges of the pedals. When the student places his foot on the pedal, the teacher connects the two ends of the strap over the widest portion of the instep. A wide strap is recommended for this purpose.

The teacher can incorporate easy-to-read traffic signs in an obstacle course for this student. The signs can be like the ones mentioned in previous sections. Constructing an outdoor bicycle course is feasible if the teacher has his program at a residential or day-training center. A special education school can also be considered if it has the space. The teacher can design a bicyle training area where he can hold classes for his students. The students can go from this area to the actual tricycle and/or bicycle course.

The teacher should keep the program simple and enjoyable for this student. What must be remembered about this student is that the severity of his condition should be considered along with his intellectual capabilities. His physical education program will mainly be geared for the retarded individual.

MONGOLISM

Physical education for the mongoloid child does not differ to any great extent form that of the educable and trainable mentally retarded student. In other words, educable and trainable retarded students are dealt with on an individual basis in relation to the perceptual skills that need to be developed or refined.

The mongoloid child needs special consideration when referring to the acquisition of basic physical skills, terminology and procedures used in the physical education program. Developing physical skills in the physical education settings is important to his relationships to other educational areas. The classroom and home are two additional learning settings where he will need to develop basic physical skills.

Equipment should be specially designed when and where needed. Various devices will be too large for this student to manipulate successfully. Smaller, less cumbersome devices will have to be devised. There will also be occasions where small devices will have to be enlarged to aid in the development of a particular perceptual skill.

The teacher should work to eliminate any perceptual deficits this student has. Gross motor activities can be developed by the use of special physical education devices. An example where special devices can be used is in the development of hand-eye coordination. Large, round sponges can be used in a ball-tossing activity instead of balls. Balloons can be utilized in an activity such as the tossing game where the student will have ample time to react to the balloon in the air. A game of ringtoss can be played with larger disks made from cardboard boxes. The teacher should be aware though, that a disk that is too large can hamper a student's efforts in the activity.

Walking, running, jumping and climbing are skills that will be used in a variety of physical education activities. Through these skills, a student can develop a higher degree of physical fitness. This is one area that the mongoloid child needs to improve to prevent obesity. Special physical fitness devices can be constructed for this student to develop all of the above mentioned skill areas. Gradually, more difficult pieces of equipment can be used in an obstacle course. One station can be where the student has to climb over an obstacle, and another station could be where he has to jump up and pull a rope that rings a bell. There can be many variations to this idea. Some other special devices are discussed in the sections on the educable and trainable mentally retarded student.

MUSCULAR DYSTROPHY

The instructor must first realize that the student with muscular dystrophy has a terminal condition. What physical skills the student has today will decrease in time because of gradual muscular weakening. We know that with such conditions as cerebral palsy, visual impairments and spina bifida, for example, the child will develop physical skills of varying degrees in a matter of time. Unfortunately, this is not the case with the child who has muscular dystrophy.

At a young age, this student is capable of taking part in the regular physical education program. As he gets older, his muscular strength will begin to diminish and he will be unable to use many regular pieces of physical education equipment. Specialized pieces must be adapted to this individual where the length, weight, size, shape and even the texture of the equipment will be modified.

The physical education program for this child will change from month to month and year to year. He will start out as an ambulatory student and regress to the use of a wheelchair. It is vital for the reader to plan a program knowing the student will be progressively less able to initiate some of his former physical activities.

As the student's ambulation proficiency decreases, various contact sports should be modified. These activities can be played with more enjoyment, success and safety from a wheelchair. Basketball, flag football, floor hockey and other sports can be adapted to meet the present physical capabilities of the student. The use of a smaller and lighter weight ball should be used in some of the above sports. This way the student will be able to throw and catch the ball with a degree of proficiency. A hollow plastic hockey puck will permit the pupil to play with greater ease of movement. A beach ball would provide a bigger and lighter weight ball to use in a soccer game, for example.

Active table and floor games should be part of the physical education program for this student. Shuffleboard can be adapted to this student very easily. First, change the size of the court, then introduce the use of a lightweight disk and the use of a hollow aluminum shuffleboard stick. The top of the disk can be covered with sandpaper for added friction and the bottom should be waxed so that it will slide more easily.

Table games should have side and end boards so the student does not have to leave his wheelchair to retrieve objects from the game that might fall to the floor. The same procedure will hold for the ambulatory student who has difficulty arising from the floor.

Bowling can be adapted to enable this student to be as independent as possible. A special ramp or pushing device can be constructed for this purpose. Devices of this type can be seen in Chapter Four with additional descriptions and discussion.

Swimming is an excellent activity for a student with muscular dystrophy. Trained personnel are needed to work with this student in the swimming program. The water will afford less resistance and permit additional freedom of movement of all four limbs. The use of adapted swimming devices should be used to aid the student in basic swimming skills and in building self-confidence. A student with muscular dystrophy can be seen in the section on swimming in Chapter Four. During the swimming activity, the student could wear four of these adapted swimming devices, one on each upper arm and one on each thigh. As he gains some proficiency, one, two or possibly all of the aids can be removed. He will need to have the devices returned to his limbs when he begins to tire. If the student is capable of performing a few strokes without the aids, he should be encouraged to do so. He should be given the experience of feeling his own body in the water, even if only for a short while.

Activities that do not require the student to use large devices should be introduced. Square dancing, movement exploration and low organizational games are excellent for this student. Different tempos of dances can be used where the student can take part without becoming too fatigued. Devices that are close to the floor in an obstacle course will permit the student to take part with a limited degree of physical effort. Easy to handle devices can also be used in an individual segment of movement exploration. This is where the students in the class each has his own device and performs with it to a set of instructions or to music. An activity such as this would allow the student with this muscular condition to execute skills on his level of physical proficiency and not be compared with anyone else.

A modified game of scooter soccer can be played by this student. This is a game where the students in the class are on flat scooters, either on their stomachs or seated with their legs out in front of them. Some students will require two scooters, one for their legs and one for the upper body. These are usually the weaker students in the class. Safety belts should be placed around the scooter and student to prevent him from falling off during the game. A large beach ball can be used in the game. The students can easily push a beach ball around the gymnasium floor without fear of injury should the ball hit them.

The physical education program can also help to delay an inevitable phase of this condition. This phase is where the student regresses from self-ambulation to the use of a wheelchair. Many physicians believe it is best to have the child ambulatory as long as possible. The physical education instructor can help the student to maintain his upright stance through adapted equipment and activities.

Special protective devices should be worn by the student who is still at the ambulatory stage but whose gait is unsteady. These devices are knee and elbow pads and protective helmets. The protective devices, combined with the adapted equipment, will allow the student to remain in his ambulatory state for a longer period of time.

Many activities can be adpated in the school setting that can also be used in the home. This is not unique to the student with muscular dystrophy, but rather a strong goal of the adapted physical education program. A high degree of carry-over of physical activities to the home is a necessity to the parents of this student. The entire family must participate in recreational activities as the student's physical skill level decreases. This is why an adapted program for this person is so very vital. The physical education program for him is a constantly changing one and needs realistic adaptations to activities and equipment. Even though the prognosis is poor for this child, he must be viewed as any other student in terms of meaningful experiences.

SPINA BIFIDA

Spina bifida is not a totally limiting condition in the physical education program. Once the student acquires the skills of using crutches, braces or a wheelchair, the scope of various activities is increased. Not all students who have this condition are confined to a wheelchair. Their need for adapted equipment will not be as great as the more physically involved student.

Many of the activities the student will take part in will be from his wheelchair. Some of these are basketball, badminton, soccer, miniature golf, ringtoss and hockey. These and other activities must be planned for on an individual basis. The student will benefit by having an adapted device for retrieving horseshoes, golf balls, hockey pucks, small balls and other similar objects. This device would help at times when he could not reach objects on the floor by himself. One such device was mentioned in a previous section where a stick was used to fit into a hole in a piece of equipment. Two pincer attachments, secured to the end of a stick, is another device the teacher could construct. One pincer arm is stationary, while the other arm is connected to a cable that fastens at the top of the stick to become the trigger. When the student pulls the trigger, the movable arm closes around the object and the student can pick it up.

Additional physical activities the student can take part in are square dancing, gymnastics, swimming and roller skating. Square dancing requires varied speeds and directions of movement. Not only is it a worthwhile activity for the young student, but a therapeutic one as well. He learns to move his wheelchair through different maneuvers at various skill levels. It is also a good activity for the student on crutches, for the same reasons.

This author has had students with this condition in various gymnastic events. Some of these events have been tumbling, trampoline work, modified vaulting, parallel bars and stunts. There are specific precautions that must be taken before any of these students can take part in activities such as these. The immediate precaution is to check with the student's physician or physical education permission form. The form should state which activities the student can or cannot take part in, and so on. If any of the previously mentioned activities are allowed, then the next step is to consult the student's physical therapist. Together, both of you can plan a safe course of action for this student. His personal safety is your first and utmost concern. It might be best if he wore his braces on some of the pieces of equipment while on others it would be best if he didn't.

Before the student goes on any piece of equipment, there are certain precautions to be taken that are of a personal nature. These should be cared for by the student himself as soon as possible prior to the start of the class. If he has a urine-collecting device, then it should be emptied before coming into class. Whatever means used to take care of waste matter should be cared for prior to class so the student or teacher does not have to stop during the class to care for this problem. Certainly emergency cases will arise and the teacher should be prepared for these.

Work on the trampoline should be conducted by a competent instructor. Even for normal students, this is a dangerous activity if not used properly. The students can execute some basic stunts on the mats before going on the trampoline. Side rolls, front drops and side drops can be performed on the mats, then transferred to the trampoline. The competent instructor can and should be on the trampoline with the student for the initial phases of his instruction. Spotting is the most important requirement of the teacher. He should protect the student's neck and back from any over-extension or weight-bearing. A small pillow can be used around the student's back for added safety. The ambulatory student can go through the same basic steps as the nonambulatory student and progress to the use of the overhead spotting belt. This piece of equipment was discussed in a previous section.

Vaulting can be executed with an adjustable vaulting box. Some of these boxes have three or four sections to them. A long mat should cover the vaulting box for added safety. One high section should be placed in front of a low section with the mat covering both and continuing down the floor. The student is assisted onto the high mat which is approximately four feet high. Then, with the help and spotting of the instructor, the student can pull himself over the top section and roll down the mat. Using or not using braces will depend on the individual student and the degree of physical involvement.

This author has been very active in swimming programs for the spina bifida student. Special precautions must be taken to insure the health and safety of this, and other students, in a pool. The student should be on a regular schedule of bowel evacuations. This schedule should be worked out at home for best results. The procedure for getting the student ready for swimming is a relatively easy and proven successful one. After making sure the student is free of bowel and bladder material, place a large plastic dry cleaning bag on the student as you would a diaper, using adhesive tape to secure the ends. The bag mentioned here is the plastic covering you would receive with your clothes from a dry cleaning establishment. These bags cling extremely well to the student, even in water. In case a student should excrete feces, the bag will contain it until the student is removed from the pool. After the plastic bag is on, put on a pair of firmly fitting rubber pants. The bathing suit goes on last. These precautions will suffice for the thirty or so minutes the student will be in the pool. The adapted swimming devices the student will use can be seen in Chapter Four with further discussion.

Roller skating for this student is an adaptable physical education activity. The device that is used is a modification of a four-point walker and a hand rail from a set of parallel bars. Regular shoe-type roller skates can be used by some students, while others will have to use the street type. In order to use either set of roller skates, the student should be able to use crutches. He should at least have had the use of a set of parallel bars in his physical therapy gait training program. These are not prerequisites for the use of the adapted roller skating device. The student should be able to maintain an upright position with assistance while using this adapted device. The teacher can hold onto the student as he learns to skate. This device is discussed in further detail in Chapter Four.

Many other physical education and recreational activities that have been discussed for some of the other physical handicaps can also be utilized by this student. The reader should search for the simplest and least time consuming piece of adapted equipment. This is the key to adapting physical education equipment to the student with spina bifida.

TRAUMATIC AND CONGENITAL AMPUTATIONS AND DEFORMITIES

The physical education teacher of the handicapped will meet students with varied degrees or causes of amputations and deformities. It is the responsibility of this teacher to make adaptations to activities with respect to each student's capabilities and interests.

In order for the amputee student to achieve any degree of success, he must first have suitable training in the use of his prosthetic appliance. The student will have been taught how to function in daily living activities while an inpatient in a hospital program for amputees. He may also be an outpatient at this hospital, while attending school, either full time or on a restricted basis. The emphasis in this section will be on upper limb amputees and equipment, with lower limb conditions being dealt with on a limited basis. This author believes that procedures and safety precautions are the necessary factors for the latter student and not primarily the need for adapted equipment.

There are certain conditions the teacher must be aware of before he adapts a piece of eqiupment to a student. First, he must know if the amputation was congenital, traumatic or a diagnosed medical necessity such as removal of a badly deformed limb. The teacher would want to know when in life the amputation occurred and was the dominant limb involved. Although the student's medical history would not appear to have any bearing on the actual construction of equipment, the reader would want to know these facts so that he could plan the most efficient piece of equipment for the student. It is very important to correlate the adapting of equipment to the prosthetic training the student has had. A close relationship with the physical therapist will help the physical education teacher in selecting the most suitable procedure or design of equipment for the student

The student who has one upper limb prosthetic device and a functional other limb, will still require adaptations to equipment. Volleyball is one such activity where adaptations will need to be made. It is best for the individual to play with two hitting surfaces. If he used his hand and terminal device, the ball might not be struck accurately. However, holding a firm section of a plastic bottle cut out so that it resembles a shield, with his device will enable the student to hit the ball squarely. The shield is light enough so that it will not hamper his playing.

Shuffleboard sticks can be adapted to the individual's prosthetic device by the use of the handle from a plastic bottle. The handle must fit firmly over the end of the shuffleboard stick. The handle can be placed at any point on the stick where the student can use it most effectively.

Miniature golf can be adapted to this student in much the same way as shuffleboard. Because all new golf clubs are metal, holes can be drilled through them without any risk of cracking. After drilling two holes at the desired point, place a small metal loop through each hole. These loops are commonly called eyelets. After they are inserted into the shaft of the club, the student's terminal device will fit into each eyelet. This procedure will allow for greater leverage and an easier means of playing the game.

The game of badminton can be played by adapting a short-handled, lgihtweight racquet similar to the way the miniature golf club was suited to the individual. This procedure will work for the individual who is a double amputee as well. A piece of Velcro material might have to be secured to the handle of the racquet to provide additional stability to the device. A tennis racquet may be adapted in exactly the same way as the badminton racquet. If the two eyelets do not work, then a U-shaped ring can be used in its place. This will also give the racquet a means of support and stability.

Table games will require less adaptations to equipment than most large muscle activities. Games that require the student to hold onto small, lightweight devices will need some modifications. Nok hockey sticks will have to have tapered ends to allow the terminal device to fit firmly on the handles of the sticks. The racquet used in table tennis can be adapted by making shallow grooves in the end of the handle. The addition of a Velcro strap to the handle will provide the student with a more stable piece of equipment.

A lightweight wooden scoop to be used for bowling can be constructed for the student with a prosthetic device. The student places his appliance through two or three Velcro straps which are fastened to the scoop. The straps are secured around the prosthesis and the platform of the scoop. The platform extends back so that the prosthesis will rest on it. There is also a hook placed on the back of the ball support for the terminal device to fit into for maximum stability. This device will greatly aid the double amputee and the individual who has one prosthetic device and a limited functional other limb.

Floor hockey can be played by adding a small plastic loop to the upper portion of the hockey stick. The loop can be from any plastic container having a handle. When the loop is secured to the handle, the student will be able to grasp it with his terminal device and hold onto the stick with his good limb, thus creating a more effective two-point grasp.

The sport of softball can be adapted to the student with a prosthesis. First of all, the size and weight of the bat will be determined by the degree of amputation, type of prosthesis and the strength in that remaining portion of the limb. The degree of proficiency of the prosthetic device will, of course, have a bearing on the type of adaptation to be made. An eyelet should be placed in the bat where it affords the student the best possible leverage and ease of movement. The eyelet should not be so large that it will cause the bat to crack. Using an eyelet with a thin shaft and large opening is most desirable. If the student is a double amputee, then two such eyelets can be used.

Catching the ball in a softball game is another concern of the student. Here, the teacher can again use a scoop, cut from a large plastic bottle, to catch the ball. The scoop can even be used to throw as well as catch the ball.

An archery bow can be adapted by adding a special extension to the grip. A solid wood or metal T is placed on the handle so that it is parallel to the ground when held in the firing position. The bar pushed against by the terminal device is in a vertical position. As the student pulls back on the bow string and pushes against the T bar with his prosthetic device, he will add to the stability of the bow. The T can be fastened on the bow by drilling a hole through the hand grip large enough for the T to fit through, but not so large as to crack or weaken the bow. The cross bar of the T should be made so it is adjustable. With this implementation the student with a prosthetic device can have complete control over the bow.

The teacher must also consider the above-the-elbow amputee in the adapted physical education program. There will be specific problems related to this student in terms of manipulation of equipment. For various activities, the student will not have time to change the position of his appliance. The prosthesis containing an elbow joint, is equipped with a locking mechanism so that the student may secure the elbow at various degrees of flexion. This student, for example, will have to lock his elbow at 90 degrees in order to play a game of softball.

Games that require the student to move his arm frequently during the course of the activity, will have to be modified so that he can play with a fixed elbow. The teacher will have to experiment with the amount of flexion needed in the arm for various physical education activities. It is up to the teacher's ingenuity to devise a lightweight, stable piece of equipment for this student to use in various physical education and recreational activities.

Most activities that require the single leg amputee to walk or run do not acutally require adapted devices. Special rules and procedures are needed in games such as badminton, basketball, softball and volleyball. Court size could be one of the modifications to a game while time limits can also be adjusted to the individual. There are some sport and recreational activities that do not require special rules or modifications. Table games are such activities along with various floor games.

The student with a lower limb prosthesis will have to observe various safety rules and precautions during active games. Indoor activities in the gymnasium will present a consistent surface to play on. Falling is the one problem the physical education teacher will have to be concerned with in regard to this individual. Outdoor activity areas will present different situations to this person. On this terrain, the student will be slowed by the resistence of the grass or other ground covering. If he were to fall on a grass surface, free of debris and holes, his chances of sustaining an injury are far less than if he were inside on the gymnasium floor.

Usually, when a student enters the adapted physical education class wearing a lower limb prosthesis, it is safe to assume that he has had prior training in its use as a means of ambulation. The physical education teacher will have to adapt previous training to specific physical education activities. The student's personal safety, along with the safety of others in the class, is to be considered. Floor hockey, soccer, basketball and flag football are some of the sport activities that require programming by the teacher to eliminate possible injuries or accidents.

Many of the known traditional activities can be adapted to students with deformed upper limbs. These deformities can include malformations to the limb, or to a certain segment such as the hand. An absence of bones or muscles in the limb or the hand would certainly be included in this section on deformities. Devices with handles will need to be fitted to the student's hand. For example, a badminton racquet handle may need to be made larger. One way in which to accomplish this is to cut a section from an old bicycle tire and fasten it around the handle. This way the handle is enlarged and affords the student a better grip. Thick foam rubber is another material that can be used for this purpose. The foam rubber on the handle will contour to the student's hand. A specially designed glove can be made that will fit the student's hand and will also hold the paddle. The glove can be secured to the paddle to afford the student the added control. This method is excellent for the individual who has difficulty in grasping slender objects.

Table and floor game activities can be adapted to these students very easily. Since many of these games do have small devices the student may need larger versions of the same pieces of equipment. A game of horseshoes can still be the same even though the horseshoe itself does not resemble the original item. Soft wood can be used to make a special horseshoe. The part the student holds onto can be cut and shaped to fit his hand. After this adaptation is made, the teacher can modify the rules of the game to suit the student's needs. Commonly used household sponges can be used in a modified game of shuffleboard. The sponges are approximately one-half inch thick and cut to the shape of a circle. The diameter of the sponge can vary according to each student's ability to hold this device. The student can squeeze the sponge for a better grasp and will not have to juggle with a piece of equipment that does not conform to his hand. The court size and shape can also be modified to the skill and age level of the students playing the game. An outdoor variation can be played with the same pieces of equipment, except that water is used. This time the court is made from an old sheet with the court sewn on it. The players dip their sponges in water and then toss them onto the sectioned-off areas on the sheet. This game is a great deal of fun for the students on hot days.

Bowling is a recreational activity that the student can take part in regardless of the deformity to his upper limb. The weight of the ball will be a factor in this activity, but this is not a problem in the physical education class where large hollow plastic bowling balls can be used. These balls are of regulation size, but not regulation weight. Holes can be drilled in this ball that will fit the fingers of the student. When the time comes for the student to use a regulation weight ball, he will have developed the needed basic skills through the use of the adapted ball. The lightest weight ball that an automatic pin-setting machine will work with is eight pounds. If the teacher can build an understanding communication with the proprietor of a bowling establishment, he might be able to receive a bowling ball as a donation. Community members might be able to help in this matter as well, with contributions of no longer used bowling balls.

The procedures and methods mentioned in this section can insure the amputee and deformed student a place in the physical education and recreation program.

NEED FOR
ADAPTED EQUIPMENT

T HE NEED FOR ADAPTED physical education equipment is as great as the indivdual's mental and/or physical handicap. There is a need for specialized equipment when the handicapped person is unable to independently initiate the activity with existing pieces of equipment, or when there is no equipment available to him. The traditional program of physical education does not meet the needs of the atypical student. His degree of physical involvement cannot be lessened by the special equipment, but the devices can lessen his limitations in physical activities.

EDUCATION FOR ALL: TOTAL PERSON

It is the philosophy of American education to educate all our citizens and to develop the total person. Each and every mentally or physically handicapped individual should receive the best possible educational experience. Whatever capabilities and interests these people have should be developed to their fullest. Physical education for these individuals should add to their personal growth. The areas of social, emotional and physical development must be the main centers of growth.

Additional education and training can open up new avenues of life encounters. It is important for these individuals to acquire the skills that are necssary for existence in our present day society. These skills should allow them to be able to communicate and relate to others in work and play settings. Being able to participate adds to one's own self-image, which is where the concept of the total person is most important.

The mentally and physically handicapped need specialized

pieces of equipment in order to realize their capabilities. The equipment can open up new areas of interest and, most of all, new outlets for leisure time activities. These people can take advantage of community-sponsored recreational sites and commercial recreational establishments. The handicapped person should see himself in areas and settings that were once inaccessible to him. This last statement assumes that the handicapped student will be able to use his newly acquired physical skills outside of the learning setting. A description of learning settings will follow later in this chapter.

INCREASED AWARENESS FOR PHYSICAL EDUCATION

State, local and federal organizations have seen the need for broader special education programs. Private groups of a nonprofit nature are also expanding their concern for a wider program of education for handicapped individuals. More handicapped children are attending schools than in the past. Daniels (1954) emphasizes that physical education contributes to the growth and development of children with disabilities. It has been noted that since World War II there has been a positive effect on the handicapped. This has come about because society has come to realize that no individual is happy unless he is able to take part in activities around him (Rathbone and Lucas, 1959).

Professional organizations such as the American Association for Health, Physical Education and Recreation (AAHPER) have many articles published in their journal pertaining to increased physical education for the mentally and physically handicapped. The AAHPER has various supplemental journals dealing with physical education for the handicapped. One is called *Challenge,* which deals with physical education and recreation for mentally retarded children. Another is entitled *Outlook,* which concerns itself with physical education and recreation for the physically handicapped. Still another is called *Programs for Handicapped,* and it deals with both mental and physical handicaps. The Council for Exceptional Children is another professional organization which is active in physical education for handicapped children. Many articles appear in its journal, relating to research and programs already implemented, on recreation and physical education for various types of handicaps. A newsletter is published by Southern Illinois University, entitled *Information Center, Recreation for the Handicapped (ICRH)*. This newsletter reports on new programs for both the mentally and physically handicapped. There are additional journals and papers which publish current trends in programming and research in the area of physical education for handicapped persons that have not been mentioned here.

An organization that is doing much to foster physical education programs on a competitive basis is the National Wheelchair Athletic Association. This organization sponsors wheelchair games in the United States and in foreign countries as well.

New books on adapted physical education for the physically handicapped, texts on instructions and planning for the mentally retarded, and this book on adapted physical education equipment are being published to inform professionals, physicians, students and parents of handicapped children of ways to instruct a handicapped person in a physical education activity.

The news media is increasing its coverage of special physical education events. One of these is the Olympic Games for physically handicapped individuals. Because of the increased awareness of the need for physical education for the handicapped, recreational establishments have been built with the handicapped individual in mind.

PARTICIPANT AND SPECTATOR

Much will be said in this book concerning the mentally and physically handicapped as participants and spectators. Simply, a participant is a person who is actively involved in the course of a specific activity. A spectator, on the other hand, is one who observes an activity either in person or through the use of television. Both forms are certainly acceptable to most individuals, but too often the handicapped are only spectators. This author believes this is the case because of the lack of suitable equipment and facilities. Each student should strive for an acceptable balance between the two. Safe and enjoyable participation will depend on the type of activity (Daniels, 1954) and the equipment to be used. Enjoyment will come when the student can use the equipment in a variety of activities.

It is held that the mentally retarded lack reaction time in physical education activities to varying degrees. Through the use of adapted devices, the student can be a more active member of the activity. Changing the weight, size and mechanical make-up of devices will allow the student to develop perceptual skills. A larger hitting surface on a racquet might assist the student who has to compensate for a slow reaction time.

The physically handicapped students need devices that are suited to their individual needs. This is not as difficult a task as some might imagine. First, the activity being taught must be considered. Next, it must be decided what pieces of equipment are needed to accomplish various tasks in the activity. From here, the instructor can visualize his students' needs and the "what and how" of adapting equipment for them. The next step is to have the student become involved through the use of specialized pieces of equipment. If the teacher hopes his students will become participants, then he must present activities that have extended leisure time value. The activities must be those the students can do when they are out of the school setting (Mathews, Kruse and Shaw, 1962).

It is very important to have any student become a good spectator. We all cannot be active participants in all recreational and sporting events. However, we should be exposed to as many as possible. Physical education must instruct students in the basic concepts of many physical activities. As a spectator, it is important to understand terminology, rules, goal(s) and basic startegies to fully enjoy the game. The mentally and physically handicapped should experience both sides of a recreational or physical education situation. Here, the author is not limiting the idea of participant and spectator to those who are classified as being slow learners, educable and trainable, but is including those who are considered infirm as well. In many cases, they too, make for good spectators while enjoying the game.

PUBLIC SCHOOL

Public schools account for the largest population of school-age children in the United States. The need for adapted equipment would depend on the number of handicapped youngsters in school. The school levels in discussion are elementary, junior and high school. There are two major trends in programming for the mentally and physically handicapped in these public schools. One way is to have a separate, self-contained classroom. The other way is to integrate them into the regular class. Whatever the system, the necessity for adapted equipment would remain the same.

The amount of equipment necessary is greater where the mentally or physically handicapped student is in a homogeneous setting. The instructor would need many variations of the same piece of equipment. The integrated system also requires that the handicapped student have adapted devices, but the amount would be less. For some, a game of badminton can be played with a regular size racquet, but for others it means playing with a short-handled, lightweight racquet. All in all, the mentally and physically handicapped student, whether in a class for the handicapped or integrated into a regular grade class, has to have usable physical education equipment—usable in the sense that he can use the devices.

RESIDENTIAL SCHOOL

The necessities for adapted physical education equipment in a residential setting for the mentally and physically handicapped are varied and, in a way, unique to this situation. In a public school setting, the carry-over value of a physical activity is to the home and community. However, the residential individual must be able to use the equipment in his living quarters, which could be a cottage, ward or room.

The equipment in this setting must be designed to reflect other areas of training, such as in the academic field. Colors, mathematical concepts, and so on, should be built into the scheme of the program of physical education. The skills the child acquires in the learning setting should be suitable for use in his living area and in his leisure time.

Residents should be supplied with sufficient pieces of equipment in their living areas. The equipment in this setting is to be simple and easy to use. Children should, in most cases, be able to use the devices without fear of failure in the activity.

Operation of the equipment should allow the residents to develop self-confidence and promote self-initiating games. The devices will have to be durable because of the extensive use they will receive. In some instances, there will have to be a duplication of devices — one set for use in the cottage and another to be used at the recreational site. In this way, the concept of total planning is in effect.

SPECIAL EDUCATION SCHOOL

Usually, this type of setting is a public school for children who are mentally and/or physically handicapped. They may range from preschool age to a chronological age of seventeen. Many times this population does not live at the school. They are transported to the school from the community and nearby areas. Classes for the deaf and hard-of-hearing, blind and partially sighted, mentally and physically handicapped are included in this school. There are schools that are designed only for blind, deaf and mentally retarded children. The school population can range from sixty to one hundred or more depending on the geographical area it serves.

The physical education program in the special education school will need devices which are geared to the age level of the students as well as their handicap. Children in the preschool class will need smaller, lighter, and easier to use devices. Equipment must be small enough so that the smallest child can handle the devices easily and effectively. These devices should prepare the students for the use of other devices in future units of instruction. On all levels, the equipment needs to challenge the student. Teachers should be able to determine the skill levels of their students in order to build a better program suited to their individual needs.

Younger children will need equipment to help them develop their basic movement concepts. These concepts are spatial relationships, speeds of movements, directions of movements, and so on. Through the use of planned activities and appropriate equipment, these students can then move to more advanced activities. These activities are those that can be found in the child's community and home. Bowling, archery, badminton, miniature golf, skating and swimming are just a few activities that the special education school should be presenting to the handicapped.

DAY TRAINING CENTERS

The population of many day training centers is made up of moderately to severely mentally and physically handicapped children. The ages of these students range from preschool to about junior high school age. Day training centers are established to help prevent the placement of a child into a residential setting. The center instructs the child in self-feeding skills, toilet training and other self-help skills.

This type of setting has to have equipment that the parents are capable of constructing and using with their child at home. Therefore, it must be inexpensive and durable. Many of these boys and girls are capable of learning team type activities which are useful within the family setting. Equipment that incorporates large and small muscle activities is vitally important to all children who are in the special education setting.

EQUIPMENT

E QUIPMENT SHOULD FACILITATE new areas of learning. In this section, areas to be discussed are the development of language skills, physical skills, mathematical concepts and more. The student should learn what responsibility for equipment means to him and others around him.

Combinations of teacher-made and commercially produced devices will be explained and ideas given in this area. One point this author would like to make is that the equipment should never take the place of an already existing physical capability; rather, the equipment should enhance the skill developed by the individual. A student who can use his own arm to bowl should not use an adapted device.

Other areas which will be discussed are storage for physical education equipment, including audiovisual aids. Sources for adapted physical education equipment will be discussed with many suggestions in this area.

GOALS FOR ADAPTED EQUIPMENT

There are immediate and long range goals for adapted physical education equipment. These goals not only affect the handicapped individual using them, but also the people he encounters. The following goals and their descriptions will present a basis for a sound adapted physical education program.

One initial or immediate goal of the adapted equipment is to develop existing physical abilities. For clarification, the term "ability" in this book is described in terms of an individual's potential to acquire or develop a new physical skill. It is assumed he has pre-existing basic skills that can be developed into a final or new skill. For example, a physically handicapped student in a wheelchair is able to rise, lower and extend his arm, but he is unable to hold a bowling ball. He has skills needed to learn how to use an adapted device. The instructor should also investigate the possibility of the student bowling out of his wheelchair, using his own limbs. The student should use all his own abilities when and wherever possible. It is when the student cannot use his own skills to execute the activity that he should use adapted devices. Probably the most important immediate goal of the equipment is to permit all students to participate in the physical education program regardless of their handicap. (Fait, 1966).

Through the use of the equipment, the student can concentrate his efforts in a positive approach to enhancing his capabilities. The equipment can aid the student in eliminating extra or overflow physical movements that cause inappropriate and unwanted physical actions. A new skill is defined by this author as the successful completion of a desired coordinated physical and mental effort that the individual could not, or did not, know how to do prior to instruction. Whatever the piece of equipment, the goal for its use must be either develop a new skill or enhance an already present ability.

When special devices are being constructed, they should be programmed for the development of other related areas. Two such related areas are mathematical and geographical concepts. Keeping score and measuring are two examples of mathematical concepts.

Geographical concepts can include up, down, behind, high, low, in front of, and so on. Many pieces of equipment will include one or more of these concepts in its description and use. By using the equipment, the student is being familiarized with the meaning of these concepts.

Special devices can afford the handicapped person a place with his own age peers. Being able to take part in a recreational event is a social outlet for this individual. As an equal part of a group, this individual can be considered to be developing along normal lines. Having the handicapped person in as many activities as possible is good for him and others as well. As an active member, he can demonstrate the capabilities he has and how he can use them.

By involving the student in physical activities which are programmed to develop physical and academic skills, he is leading to the development of interpersonal relationships. More clearly, the handicapped individual is demonstrating that he and people like him have the same interests, needs and desires for enjoyable physical activities as normal individuals do. It is hoped that nonhandicapped people will come to realize what handicapped people can do—not what they cannot do. Equipment by itself will not bring this about, but rather will enable the handicapped person to demonstrate his ability to take part in the same activities as his normal peers.

A relationship must be built in the community with people who own or operate recreational establishments. The teacher should explain and even demonstrate special devices used by his students. He should emphasize to these owners that allowing all people to use their recreational facilities is good for all and is good business.

There will also be times when the teacher will have to demonstrate a child's newly developed capabilities to the child's parents. Strained relationships might exist at home and this is one way to build or rebuild needed positive family relationships.

SOURCES FOR ADAPTED EQUIPMENT

There are many sources for adapted physical education equipment. The source may have the device already assembled or it many have the needed parts to construct a specialized device. Sometimes, the parts may not appear to be physical education equipment in themselves, but when put into use in a certain unit of instruction, they become a piece of adapted equipment.

Many of the items that make up the equipment can be found in the school, home and local community. The teacher, with his idea and design for a special device, can take advantage of the school's carpentry shop, plumbing shop, sheet metal shop and, if a school has one, a sewing room. These departments can construct almost all of the devices the teacher requests. Of course, he will have to give them an accurate description and plans for any device he wishes them to construct.

The carpentry shop is able to construct table games of all sizes, targets for ball games, miniature golf equipment and more. They can also combine their efforts with the plumbing shop and even the electrical shop to construct a certain piece of equipment. Those concerned with the use of adapted equipment should consider the construction costs and time involved in making the devices while planning and designing any adapted device.

Other sources the teacher has are the commercial manufacturers of physical education equipment. There are times when it is more economical to purchase physical education equipment from a local merchant than to construct it yourself. Less time in involved in obtaining the equipment and if any of the devices are defective, the teacher can return them at once. If the teacher realizes he needs more badminton racquets, for example, he can purchase them within a matter of days.

Teachers must order from a physical education equipment catalog when the local merchants do not have the varieties or quantities of devices he wishes. Many larger firms have a wide variety of sports, athletic and recreational equipment. A company may only deal in one type of sports or recreational equipment, such as gymnastics. The teacher can almost be assured that this type of company will have on hand the article he has ordered. One factor in the teacher's favor is the recent establishment of new companies and branches of old ones dealing with adapted physical education equipment.

The home is a good source for adapted equipment. Household articles can be used in a wide variety of units. The school's parent-teacher organization is a good place to receive donations of various pieces of equipment. Parents can collect many pieces of equipment for new games and replacements for the old ones. Some of the useful articles to be found in the home include milk cartons, plastic bottles of all sizes, cardboard paper towel rolls, sponges, tin cans of various sizes, pails, baskets, scrap wood, scrap cloth material and many more. These items are inexpensive, which makes them highly desirable.

Milk cartons can be used for bowling, target games, obstacle courses and for many types of table games. Plastic bottles can be used in much the same way, but with a wider selection of sizes. Sponges can be utilized with the milk cartons and plastic bottles for the target games or they can be used with the pails and waste baskets. One such game is having the sponge in a pail of water and the student has to take the sponge to an empty pail and squeeze the water out of the sponge. This activity would be very enjoyable in the summer months as an outdoor game. Scrap cloth material can be used on handles of badminton racquets, hockey sticks, golf clubs and on any surface where the student is required to hold onto a club or stick. These pieces of cloth material add a sense of color and brightness to the device.

Soft drink bottlers can supply a school with wooden soft drink cases. Many of these companies may be willing to donate a few cases to a school. The cases can be decorated in many ways. Their uses in target games are numerous. Many variations of the same type of game can be played without boring the student with repetition of the same game. A few games which can be played with soft drink cases are tic-tac-toe, shuffle-box, baseball, golf, and games of low organization. Disks, sponges, ball and rings can be used to play the games. The cases could be placed on tables or the floor, flat or at an angle.

Commercial recreational establishments donate used or out-of-date equipment to various organizations, schools and clubs on occasion. Local bowling establishments may have used bowling pins to contribute to the physical education program. Even though some of the pins may be slightly damaged, they are excellent for use by the physical education class. The teacher will find the pins can be utilized in bowling, obstacle courses and many other ways. After many years of use, bowling balls are ready to be replaced. The proprieter of the bowling establishment may be willing to let a school have some of the discarded balls. The balls can be used in the bowling activity in the physical education class, thereby permitting the students to have additional practice with the actual balls used at the bowling lanes.

Miniature golf courses have used balls, and even clubs that need to be replaced by new equipment. These clubs and balls can be used for more than just miniature golf. The students can use the clubs and balls in other games, drills and many versions of miniature golf.

Empty large and small thread cones can be used in the physical education program. These can be obtained from the sewing department in the school or from a nearby fabric store. Long, firm, hollow fabric cylinders can be obtained from these sources. These are the cylinders that the cloth material comes on. The cylinders can be cut to any length for miniature golf, target games and more.

The appendices at the end of the book will be of great value to the instructor. Each appendix is designed to aid the teacher in locating materials and devices in a specific area of recreation or physical education. The appendices are designed to provide a comprehensive collection of sources listed under specific headings.

TEACHER-MADE DEVICES

A teacher-made device can be one that is entirely new and created by the teacher. Of course, the teacher will modify many commercially produced devices, but the ones under discussion are those of original design or construction.

At times, the teacher will provide a diagram with size specifications for one of the construction shops previously mentioned in this chapter. It is always a good idea to include a short paragraph with the specifications of the device, stating just what the device is intended to do when it is completed. This procedure will save many phone calls back and forth between the teacher and the construction area. There are times when the instructor will make the device or game himself. This might be because he knows the special and individual needs of his students and can make slight adaptations where needed.

One of the workshops at the teacher's disposal can construct a device faster and more economincally than some commercial sources. What should be taken into account is the number of devices of one type the teacher needs and how long it will take to construct them. For separate articles, it could be beneficial for the teacher to construct them himself. For articles numbering over six, the teacher should request the school's construction shop to make them. When needed, the teacher can make adjustments to his own equipment without changing the intent or usability of the device. This is not the case with some of the commercially made devices.

Teachers will find that saving or collecting scrap material is a useful practice. Articles the teacher will want to save are plastic containers of various sizes, broken broom-handles, single grip handles, pieces of elastic, boards from packing crates, hard rubber or plastic tubing and many more. All of the above can be used in one type of device or game for many different types of students.

COMBINATION OF TEACHER-MADE
AND COMMERCIALLY-MADE DEVICES

There will be times when a teacher will add some of his own ideas to an already existing piece of physical education equipment. An example of this is in bowling. A shuffleboard stick with a small wheel added to its base will allow the physically handicapped student to bowl more easily. If a teacher has a student who cannot hold onto a regular shuffleboard stick, then a special handle would have to be added. A contoured plastic handle would be good. Shovels have the type of handle grip that could easily be added to the stick. This handle would enable the student to hold onto and push the stick with greater ease.

It would not cost the school much additional money to adapt the device just mentioned. What is intended in this section is to inform the reader that making minor improvements to a commercially-made device is a good plan. Practically no commercially-made devices are designed to be adpated to the physically handicapped. It is up to the teacher to make the needed adaptations to facilitate implementing the device.

The addition of straps and fasteners of many kinds to existing pieces of equipment is considered a combination of teacher and commercially-made devices. Having a strap attached to the handle of a badminton racquet, to enable a better grip, is an example of this type of combination.

In table tennis, the instructor could add collapsible sideboards to the table. These sideboards will enable wheelchair-bound students to play the game without having to chase the ball every few minutes or so. The need for adapted equipment is dictated by the degree of physical involvement of the individual student. There will be situations where the teacher will have to decide if he is going to combine his device with one made commercially, or construct a new device.

STORAGE

Storage of adapted devices is very different from storage for regular and normally used physical education equipment. As previously discussed, each student will have a device suited to his own particular needs. In many cases, these pieces of equipment will not be able to be stored one on top of the other, side-by-side or even on shelves. It would be a good idea to have adjustable shelves in most storage compartments. Some of the racks used for storage should be portable; that is, they should be able to be rolled from the storage area to the classroom, gymnasium, field or play area. Wood could be used to make these racks, but strong metal framing would be best. Less room will be needed for this type of portable storage unit. There should be collapsible handles on the equipment racks to permit easier storage in confined areas. Some equipment can be stored in laundry bags which can also be used to transport the devices. Using these bags will extend the life of the equipment (Rothwell, 1963).

Space for storing physical education equipment has always been a problem for many school settings. Many instructors claim there is never enough space to store equipment. One way to save space is to use the portable storage racks already mentioned. This will allow closet and shelf space to be used for equipment not in use. The type of portable storage rack or carrier is also important. For example, it is better to use a horizontal ball rack with three shelves than a ball box. The rack can hold just as many balls, but in a smaller and more orderly space. These portable racks should be narrow and be equipped with handles and wheels for easy maneuverability.

Clubs, sticks, flat ramps and other such devices should be hung in storage closets rather than placed handle or end down on the floor. Hanging equipment prevents damage to the vital parts of the devices. This is especially true for a one-of-a-kind adapted device where breakage may cause a student to be idle for a period of time, waiting for repairs to be made.

The adage, "plan ahead," is very true when it comes to storing equipment. Storage space must be considered for new and additional pieces of equipment. As new students enter the adapted physical education program, they will bring with them their needs for slightly altered, to entirely new, devices. Separate rooms for storing equipment would be ideal, but too many times teachers must settle for limited areas. Any type of storage area should insure that the equipment will retain its original shape and condition.

Where possible, permanent storage boxes could be placed inside the gymnasium area. These boxes must be placed out of the playing areas for obvious safety reasons. If there is any doubt in the teacher's mind as to the question of safety, then the boxes should not be installed.

The preceding are but a few of the guidelines for storing physical education equipment of all types. It is the responsibility of the teacher to protect and preserve his equipment so future students may have devices to use and enjoy.

The storage of audio-visual devices is handled in a similar fashion. Items that require storage space are cameras, projectors, films and filmstrips, record players, records and bulletin boards. These devices should have a safe, dry storage compartment. There should be enough room between each item on the shelf to prevent damage to the article when removing and replacing it. All of the electrical devices should have a covering of some kind for both transporting and storage. This applies to those pieces of equipment that do not have a self-contained storage or carrying case. Wires and plugs should be secured as directed in the operator's guide which is furnished by the manufacturer, and any storage recommendations should be followed. If all of these aids are the property of the physical education department, then they should be stored in a sturdy metal cabinet with a lock.

Portable bulletin boards should be stored in an area removed from any playing zone. All items should be removed from the bulletin board before it is put away. The bulletin board should then be stored against a wall—exhibition side in.

Records should always be stored in compartments intended for that purpose alone. The storage area for the records should be in sections for various types of records. This not only makes the records more accessible, but gives the teacher a quick and accurate accounting of how many records he has of each type. These are but a few suggestions to follow to insure the full life of the audiovisual aids in the adapted physical education program.

USE OF COLORS

In order to make the total physical education environment pleasant to the student, not only should the surroundings be bright, but the equipment as well. Colors can be used for more than brightening the setting. It is essential for the student to enter a colorful, stimulating and enjoyable atmosphere. The use of colors should stimulate, but not distract the student from performing in the educational setting.

Many commercial manufacturers of physical education equipment are emphasizing the use of bright colors in their equipment more than in the past. As stated in a previous section, the teacher will be constructing his own adapted devices and therefore needs to plan how he will color them.

It is true that a bowling ramp made from wood which is not colored could do the same job as a decorated one. However, if the ramp were painted red with a white arrow going down the middle toward the bowling pins, the ramp could elicit more response from the student. The ramp would not appear dull, but instead would be fun to use. The teacher could also place various words on the ramp such as STRIKE, SPARE, SPLIT, and so on. There are many ways the teacher can decorate these ramps that the students would enjoy. Having the students help decorate the ramps is an excellent idea. The one they decorate can be their's for the bowling unit.

A shuffleboard court with all black lines and numerals still serves the same purpose as one that is of two colors, but the latter is more stimulating to the student. One way the student can distinguish the numbers from the boundary lines is to print the numerals red and the lines yellow. This combination is more cheerful than the all-black court. The shuffleboard sticks could be painted to correspond to the shuffleboard pucks.

Signs, posters and bulletin boards are other objects which would benefit by a change or addition of color. When the instructor has more than one class in his program, each can have its own color of bulletin board. This gives the students in the program a feeling that the gymnasium is not just another room, but is their classroom. The color of the bulletin board should be changed for each new unit of instruction. This way, the bulletin boards do not become too commonplace in the physical education setting.

Standards are used in a variety of ways for different games. If they are permanently attached to the wall of the gymnasium, they can be painted one color. Those that are not, could be another color. Old, worn standards could be painted to give them a new appearance. The time it takes to paint these items is well worth the effort. In addition to the standards, the portable racks that hold and store pieces of equipment could be brightly painted, also. Both the racks and equipment could be of the same color or design.

There are many activities in the physical education program requiring the use of balls. The color of the ball does not help the student play the game better, but a brightly colored one will add to the excitement of the game. Many variety stores have inexpensive, durable and versatile balls that the instructor could use in his program. Some of these are two and three color combinations of various sizes. A variety of them have dots, stripes and a combination of the two. There are balls that come in iridescent colors as well. When a student comes for physical education, he doesn't have to use the same ball each time, but could choose a different one each time. These balls are lightweight and easy to handle. Like any traditional playground ball, they can be kicked, hit by a bat and thrown against a target without any damage. Because of their low price, several of them can be purchased for the price of a single all-rubber ball.

Rubber cones can be painted different colors to signify changes in directions. A red cone can signify a left turn, a yellow could mean a right turn, green could indicate the player should go over, and so on. These cones could be used in an obstacle course, wheelchair game, as well as in a track and field contest.

The largest activity utilizing a variety of colors is target games. A certain color could signify a high or low score, a good or bad hit, another player's color and so on. One target game can be played with a soft drink bottle case, large sewing thread cones and rubber rings. There are four sets of four cones each with each set a different color. Four students can play at one time, with the first one to ring all his cones being the winner. Many more target games can be designed in a similar fashion.

The teacher should remember that the use of color must be planned to accomplish a certain goal or objective for the student. The initial goal is to get the student interested in the activity. Keeping and developing his interest takes constant planning.

STUDENT-MADE DEVICES

A student-made device can be one that is entirely made by the student, one where he assembles already prepared parts, or one where he performs the finishing steps for completion of a device. Even though it is the responsibility of the instructor to furnish the adapted equipment, he can involve his students by using their creative capabilities in the construction of simple games. These games can come from home and school items.

The physical education and classroom teachers have an opportunity to combine and reinforce each other's efforts in a unit of instruction. For example, the student can make bowling pins from small plastic or milk containers in the classroom setting. This activity can be part of a crafts project in the classroom setting. The pins can be decorated by the student as he wishes, using scrap material to form many variations of a bowling pin. The student would, of course, keep the pins he makes for home or ward use. This would be the initial purpose of making the bowling pin.

Another student-made device is a scoop made from a large plastic bottle. The student can cut, paint or decorate the scoop to suit his own tastes. If the student is unable to use a pair of scissors for any reason, then the teacher could cut the bottle for him. The student could then paint the scoop with the aid of an adapted painting device. Both the physical education and classroom teachers could seek the help of an occupational therapist when it comes to adapted hand tools.

There will be those students who wish to build more complex games at home. The supervision for this would have to come from the parents. In many cases, it is best for the student to take a diagram home with him, giving full specifications and a description of the device he wishes to build. Many times, this device is one that has been used in the physical education class. For the most part, the games and devices students make or want to construct will come from the adapted program. These devices will be ones they have had fun and success with during the course of various activities.

LANGUAGE DEVELOPMENT

Each sport has a vocabulary all its own. A strike in baseball is entirely different from a strike in bowling (Fait, 1966) mentions teaching number concepts and developing reading readiness by utilizing physical activities. Within each teaching unit, the student will be using varied pieces of equipment which have dfferent functions. Not only will he increase his vocabulary of usable words and phrases from each unit, but he will also increase his ability to communicate his ideas and needs to those around him.

There are certain techniques one can use in a physical education setting to aid the child in developing his communication skills. It has been this author's practice to involve the students in a unit as much as possible. At the start of each unit, a bulletin board can be prepared, showing bright, colorful action photographs of the activity the class is taking part in at that time. This would be the teacher's bulletin board and not the one which belongs to the class. Each student would be encouraged to bring in a picture of his choice related to the activity. The picture can be from a magazine, newspaper or he can draw one using whatever materials he wishes. When he brings the picture to class, he has to tell the other students about the picture as much as he is able. He is encouraged to relate such things to the class as what the people in the picture are doing, how many people there are, what sport it is, the color of the uniforms, what numbers are on the uniforms, and more. This author has found that one or two bulletin boards for this purpose will never be sufficient.

The preceding suggestions will enable the student to fully participate in the physical education activity—both in school and at home. When and wherever possible, one subject area should strive to reinforce another. The physical education program should include the development of academic growth. Even though it is physical education, it is first an educational discipline.

UNITS OF INSTRUCTION WITH THE EMPHASIS ON EQUIPMENT

THE CONSTRUCTION OF the adapted physical education devices will enable mentally and physically handicapped students to participate in a variety of recreational and physical education activities. The equipment itself has a positive effect on the students' performances. For that reason, this chapter will attempt to describe the construction and use of adapted physical education devices.

ARCHERY

The bow used by the handicapped student has to be easily handled to be effective in this activity. This certainly applies to the student who must be seated in a wheelchair when he participates in such an event.

The student in the photograph above is using the bow in a horizontal position. The arrow is held on the bow by a special eyelet used to guide the arrow. A bow below a fifteen pound pull is preferred for the handicapped student by this author. Some sports equipment shops carry this type of bow. Other types of bows can be used and modified by the teacher to suit the needs of individual students.

The bow used by many children can be adapted to the physically handicapped by adding a metal eyelet to the shaft of the bow to guide and support the arrow. The eyelet should allow the arrow to pass through it without damaging the feathers.

The student who is seated in a wheelchair first places the arrow through the eyelet and then nocks the arrow. This is a procedure

Infirmary resident participating in an archery activity.

where the notch at the end of the arrow is placed on the bow string. A thin rubber covering can be placed around the notch of the arrow. This will give the student a better surface to grip and still allow the arrow to pass over the arrow rest and through the eyelet if one is used. Second, the student places one hand on the hand grip, which he extends, and then pulls back on the bow string with the other hand. This prepares the bow for firing. The final thing the student has to do is aim for a nearby target and release the arrow.

BADMINTON

The student in this photograph was unable to grasp the racquet, even after an attempt was made to adapt the handle to his hand in a safe and comfortable manner. This author had to resort to using wide strips of adhesive tape to securely place the racquet in a position where it could be used.

He was able to raise the face of the racquet only to the top of the arm rests. Using a lightweight racquet was imperative. A standard like the one shown in this chapter was set in front of him to use. At first there was a ball attached to the end of a string.

A severely handicapped student using a badminton racquet.

Later, a shuttlecock which is used in the badminton activity, was secured to the string. He would move his arm up and the face of the racquet would hit the ball. At first the ball was placed very close to the student so he could not avoid hitting it. This provided him with instant success in the activity. A few class periods later the ball was moved a short distance away, but it was still within his range of movement.

He participated in a game where there were two teams. The game these two teams played was similar to volleyball, but with racquets. The teacher tossed a shuttlecock toward the student from one side of a low net. If the student hit the shuttlecock over the net, he received two points. If he hit it and it didn't go over the net, he received one point. All of the students managed to receive some points for their team in this adapted badminton game.

This was a procedure that was used to individually plan for this particular student as far as equipment was concerned so that he assumed the role of an active member of the class. Each teacher

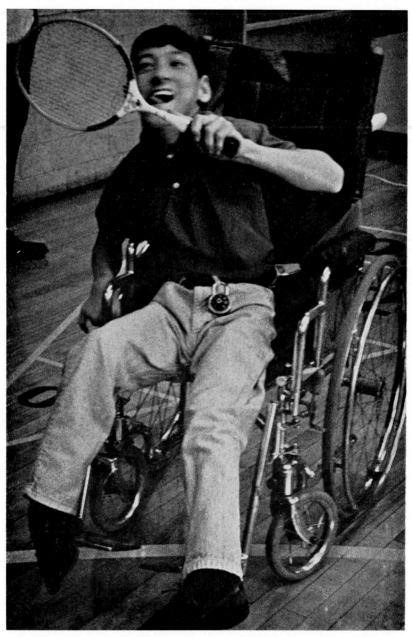

Special badminton racquet.

can use this as an example of how a severely handicapped student can be involved in a physical education activity.

This commercially-made badminton racquet is being used by a student with spastic cerebral palsy. The regulation type was too long for him to use effectively. Each time he would try to use it, he would miss the shuttlecock because the racquet was so long. Shortening the shaft of the racquet and making it lighter allowed him to hit the shuttlecock more often, as he was better able to control this short racquet.

Other handicapped students with other types of cerebral palsy conditions and muscular dystrophy, for example, found this racquet easier and more enjoyable to use than the regulation type. It truly made the difference in the badminton unit for many students.

If the teacher should have any racquets with broken shafts, he should not discard them. These can be made into safe and usable short-handled racquets. The shaft will have to be cut to the desired length and a rubber tip securely placed on the blunt end of the shaft. Several thicknesses of adhesive tape will have to be wound around the shaft for a hand grip. This procedure can also be used for broken tennis racquets as well. The teacher should never offer a racquet that he would not use himself. If it is beyond repair, it should be discarded and a new one bought as a replacement.

This author does recommend the short-handled badminton racquet for the initial phases of instruction for all handicapped students. As each student progresses, he can then advance to the use of a regulation racquet. This will depend upon each individual student, his type and degree of physical involvement, and the level of skill accomplishment.

BASEBALL AND SOFTBALL

The student in this photograph has muscular dystrophy. He is using this commercially-made device because he was unable to successfully participate in the softball activity.

The ball is placed on the top of a T which is a tightly coiled spring. The top of the spring is flat so it will support a ball. The spring is connected to a heavy metal pipe which in turn is connected to a heavy metal base. The base has a short pipe welded

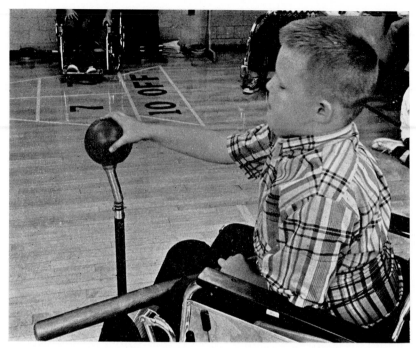

Student using a batting T.

to it. The long pipe fits down into this short pipe. This is the height adjustment for the device.

Instead of someone pitching the ball to the student, he can hit the ball off of the T at a fixed height that is best for him. Also the student does not have the speed of the ball to contend with each time it is his turn to bat.

The student is using a hollow, but firm plastic bat. This bat will certainly permit him to use whatever abilities he has to hit the ball. The rubber ball used in this game is somewhat larger than a regulation softball which makes it easier to hit off of the T.

The T, bat and ball all make the game of softball possible for the student with a muscular weakness or for one who has perceptual difficulties.

BASKETBALL

The backboard shown here was designed to be used where there is limited indoor activity space and limited storage space as

Adjustable basketball backboard.

well. The backboard slides up and down between two posts. Attached to the rear of each nine foot post is a metal strip which appears T-shaped when viewed from the top of the post. The top of the T is secured to each post all the way down. The stem of the T extends outward 1½ inches and has holes every inch for the length of the post.

There is also an eyelet attached to the top of the backboard. A strong rope is securely fastened to this eyelet which in turn passes through a pulley at the right of the top of the backboard. The rope then is secured behind the right post. This way, the teacher can easily raise and lower the backboard for the desired height. When this height is obtained, a bolt is passed thru the nearest hole of each metal strip. The bolt is hand tightened in place with the use of a butterfly nut. The backboard rests on these two bolts which prevent it from accidentally sliding down.

The main safety item the teacher should be aware of when using this device is to make sure the height of the basketball rim is at least three feet above the head of the tallest person in the game so that no head injuries occur. The students in this photograph are participating in a practice session. When they are playing a game, it would be best to separate the ambulatory students from those in wheelchairs. The rim will be lower for those in wheelchairs, but the same safety rule applies here as well. In a small gymnasium such as this one, there should be two such adapted devices for the two groups already mentioned.

The size and weight of the ball can be changed to meet the needs of each group of students. This author has used many items with handicapped students from a regulation size basketball to balloons. Small beach balls can be used in a modified game by many students. The procedure and rules of the game and practice sessions can be modified for individual students without losing the real meaning of the game.

It remains with the teacher to devise activities that all his students can take part in to their fullest capacity. Basketball is one activity that is enjoyed by many students who are mentally and physically handicapped.

The auditory goal indicator will be discussed later in terms of the implements needed to construct it and how to use it in field and gymnasium floor activities. This section will explain to the reader how to use this device in a basketball activity.

The sound originating from the goal indicator should lead the blind and partially sighted student to the spot on the backboard where the ball will rebound and go into the basket. There will be three angles from which the student will shoot the ball. These are from the right side of the basket, from the left side of the basket, and straight toward the basket. It is up to the teacher to tell the student where he is in relation to the basket. The reader is reminded to give the student as much feedback as possible. When the student is told he is on the right side of the basket, he will know he will have to shoot slightly to the right of the goal indicator. The same system would have to be employed for the other two directions.

The shooting fundamentals for the blind and partially sighted student will not have to be changed to any great degree from those of the sighted student. This student will have to practice basketball fundamentals to develop a muscle memory of each skill. That is, he will have to practice each skill so he can do it the same way

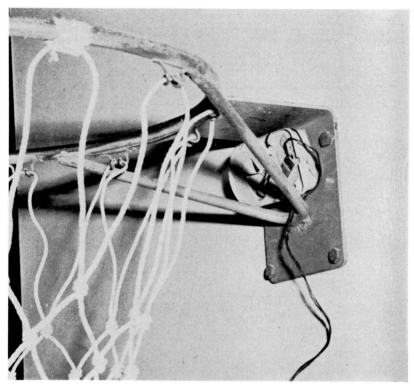

Auditory goal indicator used in basketball.

each time. Feedback is extremely important during this phase of the student's training.

When the student is ready to shoot, a sighted student can ring the bell. The shooting method just described can be used. This would be true for a practice session or for a game situation.

Two of these goal indicators could be used if the gymnasium or field was large enough. The sounds coming from each indicator should not confuse the student using them. What could be done in a situation where the teacher is in a small area would be to use a bell at one basket and a buzzer at the other. This system could even be used inside or outside where the teacher has enough space, but wishes to separate two playing areas by sound. The system used will depend upon the teacher, his class size, and the facility he must use for his instruction.

BOWLING

Push-type bowling device.

This device allows the student to push the bowling ball with great ease. An eight pound to a sixteen pound ball can be used with this device by many handicapped students. It is constructed mainly from scrap materials. Each wheel is from an old discarded hospital bed and the rubber hand grip is from a no longer used utility cart. The wood was obtained from the scrap pile in the carpenter's shop. The two four-inch bolts were obtained from the carpenter's shop as well. The handle had to be cut to length from a longer piece of aluminum pipe. The cost will certainly be somewhat higher for the teacher who cannot obtain the parts in this manner.

The platform is approximately twenty inches long and twelve inches wide. The aluminum handle is fifty-four inches long with a slight bend in the middle. The handle has this bend because the hand grip would be too high for the student to use this device effectively. The back of the platform is six inches high, while the front is four inches high. This allows the force of the push to be centered down toward the front of the device and toward the ball.

The device is placed in front of the student and slightly to one side, aimed at the pins. His hand is on the hand grip which is to the side and slightly above his shoulder. The ball is then placed in the semicircular section of the platform. The next step is for the student to straighten his arm, thus pushing the handle forward. A slow and steady motion is desirable rather than a hard, quick push. The hard push will cause the device to go to one side and make the ball miss the pins.

Aiming adjustments are needed after each push of the device. The teacher will have to work on the right combination of aiming points and speed of the push. The weight of the ball will also be a determining factor. Each student will bowl differently with this same device for various reasons. This can be worked out in the school before the class comes to the bowling lanes. The teacher should always emphasize slow and steady movements of the device for maximum performance.

The bowling ramp presented below is primarily for classroom use, but it has also been used successfully at a regulation bowling lane by handicapped students. It is fourteen inches high and four feet long. The slope of the ramp should be over three feet in length. There should be enough space for the bowling ball to rest on top of the ramp so it won't roll down the ramp when the student is not ready to bowl. Rubber pads should be placed on all surfaces that touch the floor for two reasons. First, the rubber pads will keep the ramp from sliding back or to one side when the ball is pushed down the ramp. Second, the pads will protect the floor surface. This is especially important to the teacher when he attempts to convince the proprietor of the local bowling lane to let him use the adapted device in his establishment.

Wood molding can be used on the ramp to guide the ball straight toward the bowling pins. It would be best if the ball just touches the flat surface of the ramp as it rolls toward the pins. This means that the guide rails, which are the inner pieces of wood, should be placed just far enough apart so the ball will roll down the ramp more easily.

The ramp should be heavy enough so it will remain stationary

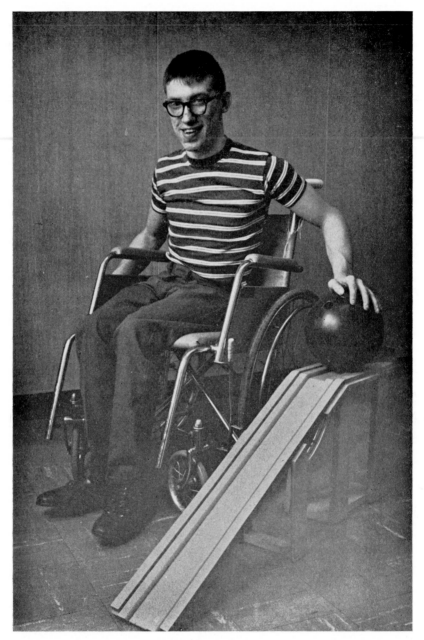

Bowling ramp.

on the floor when used, but light enough so the handicapped student can maneuver the ramp in a variety of aiming positions by himself.

The bowling scoop is twenty-one inches long and 10½ inches wide. The ball placement section is 8½ inches deep. The arm rest is one foot long, measuring from the back of the scoop. The hook where the terminal device is placed is one inch wide. It is placed in the middle of the back of the ball scoop, 1½ inches from the base, as seen in the photo below. This hook is necessary so the terminal device will be secured and keep the prosthetic appliance from moving about. The two Velcro straps are placed at two and six inches from the back of the scoop. These straps fasten around the prosthetic device for added stability. The wood used in this device is half-inch plywood, but quarter-inch plywood was used for the sides of the ball placement section.

The scoop can be used by an individual who has two upper limb prosthetic appliances and can also be used by an individual who might have one prosthetic device and physical anomalies of the other limb.

The student should spend some time developing basic skills leading up to the actual use of the scoop with a regulation bowling

Bowling scoop for student with prosthetic device.

ball. This individual should first develop coordinated movements of his arms and legs. He should practice using a rubber playground ball comparable in size to a bowling ball. The delivery can be from a standing position without the traditional step approach. The student should practice with a plastic practice bowling ball, already discussed in this book. Regulation size pins should be used throughout each practice session. The pupil should also be moving further away from the pins as his delivery skills improve. If the gymnasium the teacher is working in is too short, he can use a hallway in the building. This has been done many times by this author for students who are ready to bowl at a regulation lane. Having the understanding and cooperation of fellow teachers is very important if the practice sessions will be near other classrooms.

The individual with a prosthetic device will have to lock his elbow in a ninety degree position to use the scoop. After the bowling device is secured in place, the student slides the bowling ball from its storage place into the ball placement section. An eight pound ball is recommended by this author for the beginning student who is ready to bowl at a regulation bowling lane. The front edge of the scoop is tilted up until the time of delivery when it is lowered toward the floor and aimed at the bowling pins. The student must bend at the knees when he slides the ball off the scoop. The arm without the scoop attached is underneath the scoop for added support in aiming the ball.

These are the steps and methods the teacher can take in order for the student with a prosthetic appliance to be able to bowl. Possibly the size of the scoop will have to be changed for certain individuals, but the basic construction should be satisfactory.

There are those times that a gymnasium will be less than desirable in size for some physical education activities. The teacher should learn how to make the best of the situation and use all available space.

In this photograph below, three different modes of bowling are being conducted. Students are bowling using their own hands, bowling boards and a bowling ramp. Not observed is the bowling ramp which is being used at the far end of the gymnasium. The individuals in this picture are being assisted by their teacher and one teacher assistant. Those students who require assistance are placed at one end of the gymnasium, while the more independent students are at the other end. All students should receive aid and assistance from the teacher regardless of their degree of physical involvement. This system will allow the teacher to spend more time with those students who need the extra aid.

The physically handicapped people in the next photograph above are all from one infirmary in a residential setting. There are actually three different types of devices being used in this bowling activity. Two can be seen here and the third is a bowling ramp which can be seen in another illustration. The two that are visible here are the bowling board and the shuffleboard stick.

The bowling board is thirty-five inches long and nineteen inches wide. The guide rails, which are one inch high, are six inches apart at the bottom of the board and seventeen inches apart at the top of the board. A curved section is cut from the board. This allows the individual to push the ball off his lap or knees onto the board with greater ease than if there was no cut-out section. Using the board without the cut-out section created great

Bowling activity in the gymnasium.

Infirmary residents bowling with various adapted devices.
(Photograph courtesy of Tuscola County Advertiser, Caro, Michigan)

difficulty when the student attempted to push the ball over the edge of the board.

There are two heavy ropes attached to the top of the board which are tied to the wheelchair. This keeps the board from slipping down or to one side when the ball is pushed down the board. As the student pushes the ball off his knees, it falls onto the board and is guided straight toward the pins at the other end of the bowling lane. The student has been instructed in how to aim the board to get the best results from it. This was practiced in the school's gymnasium prior to coming to these regulation lanes as seen above.

Five students in the photograph can be seen using shuffleboard sticks to bowl with. For various reasons, these individuals could not bowl using their own arms and hands, but did not need the use of the bowling ramp or board. They all had the capability to push a shuffleboard stick with a bowling ball in front of it.

The ends of the sticks are taped so as not to damage the proprietor's lanes. The aide in this picture is placing a bowling ball down in front of one of the students to be pushed. When the ball comes to a complete stop, the student extends his arm toward the pins pushing the ball forward and causing it to roll. Students must practice keeping the end of the stick down on the floor until the ball is completely away from the end of the stick. Bringing the end of the stick up too soon will cause the ball to roll to one side or the other and go into the gutter. The reader can also see that some students can use a short-handled stick while others need a long-handled stick.

The instructor should have the student use whatever implement makes bowling the easiest, whether it's a bowling shield used on a forearm or one of the adapted devices seen here.

This bowling table game is an excellent teaching device to use in a unit on bowling. It can be used as a learning instrument at a teaching station while some of the students in the class are using bowling balls and pins of regulation size. This device has many of the same academic and physical skill principles connected to it as does the actual game of bowling.

Commercially-made table bowling game.

As the reader can see, the student rolls the ball toward the pins to score points. The pins are forced upward as the ball strikes them. After the ball reaches the back of the pin area, it will roll toward the student by itself. When any of the pins are pushed up as they appear in the photograph, all the student has to do is squeeze too levers together in front of the game and the pins are forced down to their original position. Little effort is required of the student to perform this task.

Side boards should be added to the playing table for the student who has difficulty in catching the ball when it returns from the game ramp. Additional assistance can be afforded the student by having the ball attached to the table by use of a string. In this way, the chance of the student missing the ball is diminished considerably.

This game can be used in the physical education class, recreation program, and most important, in the student's home with his family and friends.

HOCKEY

Auditory goal indicator.

The auditory goal indicator appearing in the illustration above is an easy and simple device to construct. It consists of an eighteen volt vibrating electric bell, a step-down transformer and a push-button switch. The length of wire from the transformer to the bell will be determined by the activity in which it is used. This author recommends a length of ten feet. A ten-foot length will permit the goal indicator to be used in a variety of sports activities with safety to all students who must rely on its use. The cost of this device is very low when compared to some commercially-made devices.

The teacher has the option of using a push-button switch or a knife switch. Both switches work very well, but the knife switch will allow the bell to ring continuously. With the push-button switch, someone has to hold it down to make the bell ring. All the student or teacher has to do is close the knife switch and the bell rings. Each of these switches has a place in physical education activities for blind and partially sighted students.

All of the electrical implements can be purchased from an electrical supply firm or from a local hardware store. The instructor can use any solid piece of wood to mount this device on. He can enclose the transformer and some of the wires in a small wooden box. The excess wire can be wound around two hooks placed on the side of the box. The switch can be on top of the box, where it is easy to get at and use. Constructing it this way is ideal for storage and transportation.

The plug-in auditory goal indicator can be used for a variety of activities, but is limited to indoor use where they are electrical outlets. The following section will inform the reader in how to construct a portable indicator using some of the same implements which were used in the plug-in type.

The portable auditory goal indicator consists of a six volt battery, a bell that will work off of a six volt battery and a switch. A series hookup should be used to make the device work. It should be constructed in a fashion similar to the previous type. The small wooden box with the two hooks on the side and the switch at the top should also be made for this device.

The portable goal indicator can be utilized with many outdoor activities such as soccer, field hockey and softball, to mention a few. It can also be used on outdoor basketball courts.

If the teacher does not have enough students in the class for one of them to operate the switch, the teacher should close the knife switch and let the bell ring continuously. This way, the teacher is in the activity and all students are taking part.

Should the teacher have any questions as to the construction of a plug-in or portable goal indicator, he should contact the electrical shop at his school or confer with a local electrician. It is very important that these devices be safe and reliable for student and teacher use.

The students with the hockey sticks are going through some practice drills on scoring and goal defending. The sighted student in the class is ringing the bell, giving the blind female student a point of reference to aim toward. The goalie knows that the plastic puck will be coming toward his stick, because the goal indicator is behind him. As the student hits the puck toward the goal, the goalie pushes his stick forward to push or hit the puck away from the goal. The instructor in the photograph is explaining the skills involved in being a goalie and also how to aim the puck toward the goal.

The puck must go through the plastic bottles to be a goal, but

Sighted student using auditory goal indicator for blind students.

Plastic bottles and slant-sided food container used in floor hockey game.

not above the top of the bottles. This system diminishes the possibility of head injuries to the goalie to a major degree. This way, the student who is shooting the puck toward the goal and the sound of the auditory goal indicator has to try to slide the puck toward the goal on the floor. A slant-sided food container should be dealt with in this same manner. The goalie has a better chance of defending the goal for his team without sustaining any injury to himself. This method was used by this author with much success and no injuries to any of the students.

Many other variations of the game and rules can be devised by the reader, depending on the number of students, their handicaps and the equipment they have to use.

The students in the photograph above are using common household items in a hockey game. The two large bottles, which are filled with cement to a level of two inches, are used for the goal boundaries. The puck is a food container with two bells inside.

In this pre-activity session, there are two blind students and one sighted student with spastic cerebral palsy. The cerebral palsied student is seated in the wheelchair. The student who is standing is practicing shooting the puck at the goal which has an auditory goal indicator behind it out of the photograph. A sighted student from the class is working the switch to the indicator.

The student who is the goalie is also practicing the fundamentals of his position. For this game, he is permitted to use his stick, hands and feet. His teammate in the wheelchair is practicing blocking the puck from entering the goal.

When the students are ready to play a game, the goalie will wear protective glasses, knee pads and elbow pads. The standing students will wear shin protectors, as will the students in wheelchairs. Handguards will be worn by all. These handguards are converted shin guards modified to be worn on the top surface of the hand and wrist.

When the slant-sided food container is hit, it will roll on its side or slide on the top or bottom for a short distance. The food container will roll around on its side in a circle, thereby staying close to the students. They will spend less time chasing after it and more time hitting the puck.

Different sizes of food containers can be used in a hockey game. The bigger the target, the easier it will be for the visually handicapped student to hit the puck. It would be best to start a game with the largest size of food container and proceed to a smaller one as the students gain a higher degree of proficiency in the game.

The preceding were some of the ways the plastic food containers and plastic bottles could be used in a floor hockey game with visually handicapped and sighted students. It rests with the reader to devise other variations of the games already mentioned. This will, of course, be determined by the needs of the students in the class.

As the reader can see in Figure 16, new brooms are not needed to play broomball. The students in this photograph are from a residential facility for the mentally and physically handicapped. At this facility, many brooms are used by the housekeeping and maintenance personnel. When the brooms can no

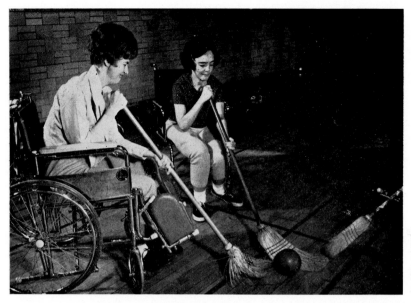

Deflated ball used in broomball game.

longer be used by these departments, the physical education teacher can use them for his program. The handles of the brooms may have to be shortened for various students so they can use them effectively. It would be a safe procedure to round off the ends of the brooms to prevent any injury to the student using the broom or to those around him.

The ball used in this game should be deflated for those students in wheelchairs, for those on crutches and for those students who cannot move about quickly. A slant-sided food container can also be used in this game, similar to the way it is used in the floor hockey game. The teacher can also use a goal net for the game, but if one is not available, large plastic bottles can be used for the goal.

Students in wheelchairs should play on smooth surfaces where they can move about easily while using their brooms and chairs. This applies to those students on crutches as well. The deflated ball, large but lightweight broom, and smooth surface will permit the student to enjoy an additional physical education activity.

Basic safety procedures and practices should be used while

playing this game. Those students who are able to maintain sitting balance in a wheelchair may remove the side armrests on their chairs. These students should definitely wear seat belts if they are to play this way. They must also have exhibited the physical ability to remain in a seated position during some other time prior to this game. Shin guards would be a desirable piece of equipment for the student to wear during the game.

If all of these safety procedures are implemented and the rules of the game are geared toward the students, it is a logical assumption that those involved in the activity will learn needed skills for other activities and, most of all, have fun doing it.

FISHING

The device seen in the illustration above was designed by Sal Muley, Director of Special Events for Garcia Corporation. It was primarily designed to be used by upper limb amputees and those who must function from a wheelchair. This author can recommend this device to be used with other physically handicapped students as well. It is feasible for the "Handi-Gear" to be used by students with muscular dystrophy, neurological conditions, upper limb amputations and deformities. Some or all of these students with these conditions will have to receive some degree of assistance from the teacher at one time or another in one of the phases of the operation of this device.

This device is made of lightweight aluminum with a fishing rod holder attached to the front of it. The holder fastens to straps which go around the individual's back and shoulders as seen above.

If the student is unable to make a cast, the teacher can do it for him. After the cast is made, the rod is placed in the rod holding tube. Casting is not necessary when fishing off a dock and the student can release the fishing line into the water by himself. There is a slot on the holding tube to lock the rod and reel in place. This applies to those reels which have a trigger as seen on the one in the photograph.

The "Handi-Gear" will permit the handicapped student to devote his time and efforts to catching a fish. It eliminates trying to hold onto a rod that is either too heavy or cumbersome for

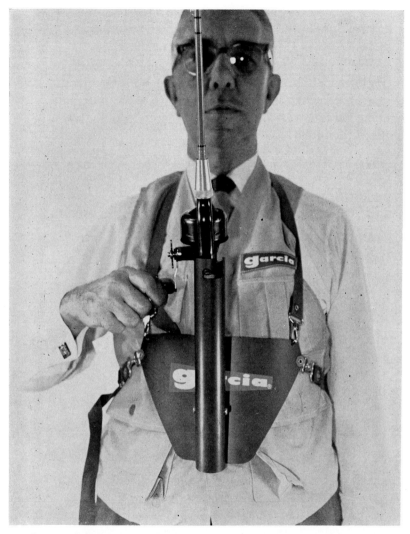

Adapted fishing device for amputees and students in wheelchairs. (Photograph courtesy of Garcia Corporation, Teaneck, New Jersey)

him. Certainly, it allows the student to be more independent. Any device which will permit the student to take a more active role in the activity is of great value to the student in terms of an additional recreational activity.

GAMES (TABLE AND FLOOR)

There is one difference between the table shuffleboard game and floor version, this being the means of retrieving the pucks. In the table game, the students do not have to use a suction cup stick. They can use one adapted device to slide the pucks back to them. This device consists of a short broom handle with a rectangular piece of wood attached to the end of the stick so it resembles a garden hoe.

Rubber sheet shuffleboard court used as a table game.

As the reader can see in the photograph above, a large table is required for this particular shuffleboard game. Smaller sheets can be used for the game court and thus a smaller table will be needed. A table-tennis table can be used for one large game or for two small courts. The size of the class and the types of handicaps will influence the arrangement of the shuffleboard courts. Facilities and equipment will also have a bearing on the types of courts used in the physical education class.

The rules for this game can be similar to those of the floor version. Each teacher will need to vary the rules to suit his students and their needs. It would be best if the rules established for the game promoted independent play by the students. This is a factor the teacher should keep in mind before he makes any rules for a particular activity.

The regulation courts and the floor and table games can be used as teaching stations at the same time. This would be especially true if there are not enough regulation courts and equipment. At predetermined time intervals, groups of students can move from one station to the next. This provides each student an opportunity to use one of the shuffleboard game variations. Each court can have a different set of numerals on it as a variation in the game.

Small squares can be placed on a sheet, each square having a letter inside of it. One set of letters can be red and the other could be yellow. The pucks and the letters should be formed in a shuffleboard court formation, but the teacher can use any variation to the game court he wishes. The red and yellow letters could constitute a word that the students can spell when they recognize each letter on the court. A word associated with this particular game can be used, or any other word the teacher chooses that his students know.

To score this particular game, each letter could be worth two points. After all pucks have been tossed, the person to guess the word formed would receive five points. This is just one variation for the use of a rubber sheet in the physical education program for handicapped students.

The individual in the photograph above has severe contractures on one side of his body and has limited hand function on the other side. By adding the handle from a firm plastic bottle to the hockey stick he was able to play at this game. The plastic handle fits firmly around the student's hand, enabling him to hold this implement with a degree of ease. When the plastic handle was added he could hold onto the stick and play the game without having the stick fall from his hand.

The teacher should make sure that the nok hockey stick does not move around in the plastic handle, but fits firmly into it. The stick can be adjusted in the handle to any angle suitable to the student's playing position.

If the teacher wishes to permanently fix the stick into the

Firm plastic handle section attached to a nok hockey stick.

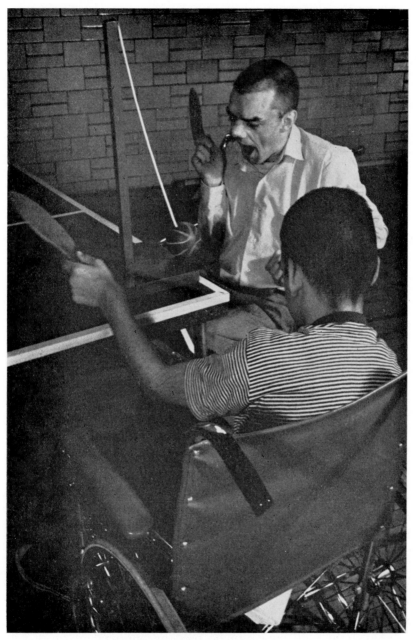

Portable table tetherball game.

plastic handle, he should first place some glue on the two surfaces and then hammer in two small nails, one on either side of the stick. The glue and the nails will securely hold the stick in place. This device, then, will be for a particular student to use when he comes to the physical education class. The student's name should be plainly written on the stick if there is more than one of these devices in use at the same time. The stick should be placed in a storage compartment where the student can obtain the device by himself. There should be a duplicate device and hockey game for him to use at home, on the ward, or in his cottage during his leisure time.

The teacher should make sure that the edges of the plastic handle are smooth and rounded before the student uses it. After it is cut from the plastic bottle, the teacher should trim the edges so they are smooth by using a piece of fine grain sandpaper. This final procedure will assure the teacher that the student can safely use this device. This procedure should be explained to anyone else who might make such a handle for a student at home or in his cottage.

The tetherball game pictured above is constructed from solid pieces of wood. The base is $10\frac{1}{4}$ inches long, nine inches wide and approximately $1\frac{1}{2}$ inches thick. The post is one inch wide on all sides and is eighteen inches tall, measuring from the top of the base. There are no nails used in this device to secure the post to the base. The post fits into the base through a tightly fitting hole slightly smaller than the post. To make sure the post would stay firmly in its place, glue was added around the edges of the hole and the post. After allowing the glue to dry for the prescribed time, the post was driven into the hole with a rubber mallet. This method of securing these two parts together has proven to be successful in terms of durability of the device.

Four small rubber suction cups were added to the bottom of the base to help hold it firmly in place. A hard pull will remove the base from the table. A strong string was nailed to the top of the post and a ball was secured to the end of it. Balls as large as softballs can be used with this stand.

The tetherball game can be used by one student or two as seen here. It is used to help the student develop hand-eye coordination for a game of table tennis or any other similar game. The students here are using table tennis paddles to play the game. They could also use their hands to catch the ball and throw it back to the other player. One student can throw the ball with his right hand and catch it with his left and then repeat the sequence for several attempts.

This device is ideal to bring to bedridden patients who can not function out of their beds for any length of time. In short, it is an excellent portable physical activity device for severely physically handicapped individuals and less involved persons to use during leisure time periods.

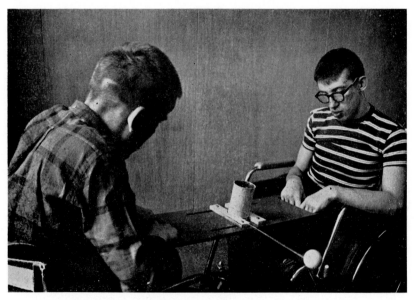

One and two man "pop can" board.

This board is twenty-eight inches long and 8½ inches wide. The handles are 1½ inches wide and seven inches long. Each slot in the middle of the board is five inches long and is for the adjustment of the can size. The small boards which hold the can in place are seven inches wide and have a semi-circle cut from the inside to fit around the can placed in the middle. Metal screws and butterfly bolts are used to hold the small boards in place around the can. This will allow the teacher to easily and quickly change from one size of can to another.

The ball attached to the can in this photograph is secured around the bottom of the can. The idea is to swing the board back and forth and "pop" the ball into the can. The teacher should start the students with a large can, short string and a small ball. This way, the students can easily swing the ball into the can. As each student develops greater skill at this hand-eye coordination activity, he can use a smaller version of this board.

Many physical actions are brought into play while the student uses this board. He has to coordinate each arm swing with that of his partner. One strong student can be paired with a weaker one. The boy at the right is leading the boy at the left. The swing is slow and rhythmical and permits the weaker student to develop some gross motor movements with his upper limbs.

Visual perception skills can be developed by both students as they use the board together or by one student playing the game alone. The use of this board, and additional visual training devices, will aid the student in other activities which require him to use hand-eye movements in a coordinated physical effort.

The equipment used in the illustration below is discarded bedding material and scrap wood. The court itself is a rubber sheet and the ends to the sheet are thin blanket scraps. The blanket ends are for nonseated students to stand upon in order to keep the sheet flat. The student in the wheelchair places his front wheels on the court to help hold it in place.

The reason for using a rubber sheet is that it can be easily folded, transported and stored. It is also easy to paint a variety of shuffleboard courts on the sheet for various groups of students. Both sides of the sheet can be used. One side can have a shuffleboard court with numerals from zero to five and the other side can have numerals of any other combination. Mathematical fractions, such as $1/4$ and $1/2$ can be used on one of the sides of the sheet for students who can add these fractions.

The shuffleboard pucks are from scrap plywood, one quarter of an inch thick. A small piece of rubber from a tire inner tube should be placed on each side of the puck to keep it from sliding

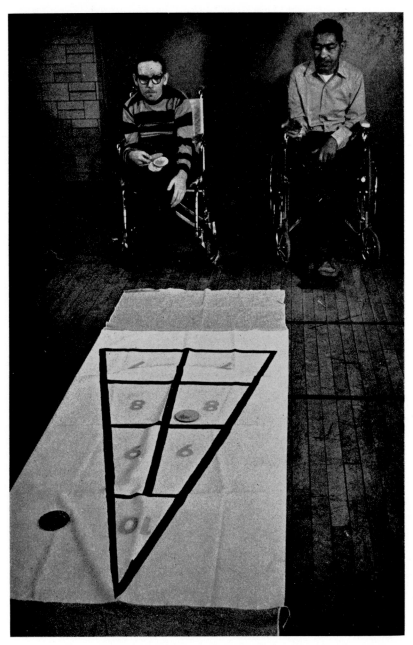

Rubber sheet floor shuffleboard game.

Floor tennis game.

Wide pieces of bedding material or rubber sheets can be used to make very simple pieces of physical education equipment. Once again, the teacher is encouraged to use whatever materials he can find for special adapted physical education devices.

This game board is constructed from a piece of solid wood, two sections of a discarded broom handle and four empty thread spools. All of the playing items are made from wood including the rings, which are commercially made. There are two sets of rings, each set a different color. The pegs and rings are of matching colors and numbers.

The procedure of the game is for each student to toss his rings onto his color peg to receive points. Should he toss his ring on his opponent's peg, the points then go to the other player. This is only one method of scoring this game and other methods can be used.

Many variations of shapes and sizes of ringtoss games can be made by the teacher for both mentally and physically handicapped students. Each game board should have predetermined objectives and goals of the effect they are to have on the student's performance. Certainly, hand-eye coordination and depth perception are being developed in this activity.

Rings can be made from materials other than wood. Firm pieces of cardboard can be cut to any dimensions that will suit individual students. Bottom pieces of plastic bleach bottles can also be used. Here, the teacher should cut the bottom of the bottle so it is as flat as possible. Then, any size hole that will fit over the size of pegs being used can be cut in the flat piece. Bean bag rings can also be made. The bean bag ring is easy to make using two pieces of cloth material of any type. Any size ring can be used that a student could hold in one hand.

Ringtoss games need not lie flat on the floor, but can have built-in standards so they will stand by themselves. In this way, the student is able to retrieve his own rings. This type of ringtoss game could be used as a floor game and a table game as well.

One ringtoss game that can be made has rings of different shapes. Some of these shapes can be circles, triangles and squares. Each should be a different color to correspond to an exact duplicate shape painted on the board and as a part of the peg. The peg should be the same color as the ring. This will help the student locate the appropriate peg. There should not be so many pegs on the board that it is difficult for the student to distinguish his colored shape from another one.

Empty thread cones glued on a piece of plywood can be used for this game as well as many scrap items found in the home and school. Small juice cans and empty paper towel rolls can be used as the pegs in a ringtoss game, to mention a few. Larger items found in the home and school can be used for a vast variety of games such as this one. If the teacher will look around the school and take a few moments each day to plan a new game for his students, his program will be enjoyed by all the students while they are developing many needed physical skills.

GOLF (MINIATURE)

Student-made miniature golf station.

The curved miniature golf station pictured above is eight feet long, twenty-seven inches wide and three quarters of an inch thick. The side molding on the edges of the board is one inch high.

This author has designed this piece of equipment to be used as a station in a wheelchair obstacle course. The end piece of molding folds down for the wheelchair obstacle course and can be fastened in an upright position for miniature golf. In this way, one piece of equipment can be utilized for two separate activities, thus saving on storage space.

The blank spaces on the board are where pieces of molding can be placed. The molding is fastened to the board with metal bolts that are secured on the bottom of the board. One, two or three pieces of molding can be added to make the miniature golf and obstacle course activities more of a challenge to individual students. The slanted edge of the molding is to face toward the student when he is hitting the ball and moving his wheelchair over the board. The height of the pieces of molding can be varied depending on the skill levels of the students in the class.

There were three students involved in the construction of this device and the one in the following photograph. One child was mentally retarded. A second was brain-injured—partially sighted and a third was a spastic quadriplegic with cerebral palsy. The teacher supervising the project cut out the basic pattern for each board with the assistance of two of the students. The students then put the finishing touches on the board, which included sanding, putting the molding on the edges and painting. Their project was for themselves and other handicapped students to use.

Many other small obstacles can be placed on the board in the form of very small tunnels, ramps and pieces of wood blocking the hole. The teacher will certainly now be able to devise his own adaptations to this adapted device. There is only one point that the teacher should remember, and that is that these small obstacles on the board must be easily removable if the board is to also be used as an obstacle for wheelchairs.

The student in the photograph above is using a miniature golf station designed by this author and constructed by the same group of students who made the curved one in the previous photograph. This board has the same dimensions as the other one, except that it is two feet shorter.

As the reader can also observe in this photograph, there are blank spaces on this board for three pieces of molding to be used in the same way as with the curved board.

At the end of the board there is one section of a hinge. The

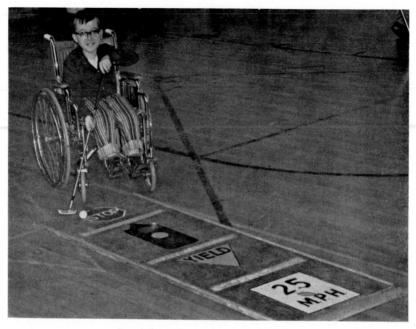

Straight miniature golf station.

other part is on the curved golf station. When the two stations are connected together, they become one large board. It can be used for both miniature golf and a wheelchair obstacle.

There are many possibilities for use of these devices and the teacher can devise numerous small obstacles to place on the boards for miniature golf. The teacher will find that there are numerous ways in which these boards can be adapted to each student in the program.

HORSESHOES AND SHUFFLEBOARD

This student shown above is using rubber horseshoes and a sliding board. The mat at the bottom is rubber to help hold the board in place and keep the horseshoes close to the pin.

The horseshoes are placed on the edge of the student's knees, aimed for the metal pin at the bottom of the board. With his right hand, the student pushes the horseshoe off his knees and forces it to slide toward the pin. As the reader can see, the horseshoe will hit the mat or pin depending on how it is situated on the board.

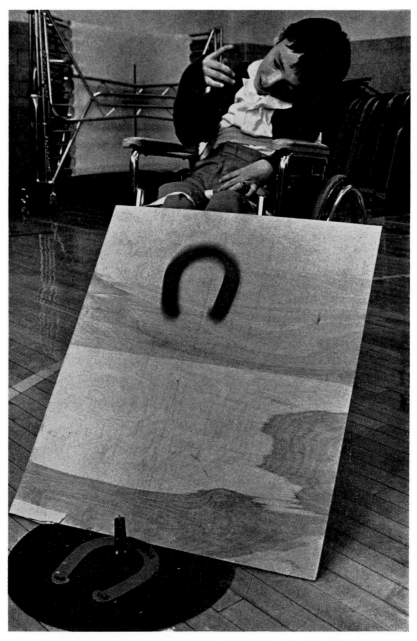

Horseshoe game for a severely handicapped student.

Any scoring system can be used, choosing from the variety of systems already discussed in this book. The teacher can add to this list by making up some of his own.

As the student begins to become proficient in this method, the horseshoe can be moved further back on his knees and slightly to one isde. Now the student has to move the horseshoe so it will slide toward the pin, utilizing the aiming techniques he was taught. A lap tray can also be placed on the student's lap with the horseshoe on it. Whatever method is used will be determined by the student's degree of physical involvement. An optimum performance system should be developed for the student who is severely handicapped.

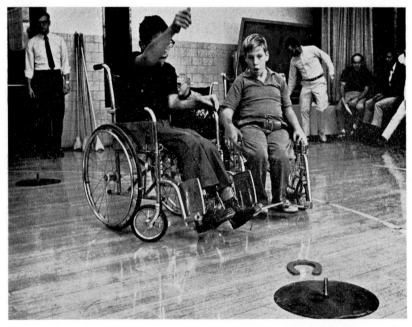

Horseshoe activity.

These two students are using rubber horseshoes along with a rubber mat. Note the distance the boys are from the standard. By being this close, each student is assured of scoring a point in each round played. This is because the scoring system is modified and suited to them.

The rubber horseshoes do not slide or bounce very far; therefore, the students do not have to chase after them. As each student develops his skill in this game, he should move further back from the pin. Of course, the distance the student moves back should be determined by the teacher as he views the student's performances. On some occasions, this author has found that the students themselves know how far to move back to where they can still score some points in a game. They do find their own optimum range by experimentation.

This activity is an excellent one to be used in the leisure time in school, in the home or in the cottage of a residential facility. The game of horseshoes does not require many complicated pieces of equipment nor does it call for any great amount of time to set things up.

Special horseshoes can be made from wood, foam rubber, several layers of cardboard and scrap pieces of plastic material. Special horseshoes can be made so a section of one fits the hand of a student with a deformity. Another one could be larger than most for a student with vision difficulties. Still others can be made so they are lighter than most for students with muscular weakening conditions. Whatever the condition, some adapted device should be developed so all handicapped individuals can play this game.

This severely handicapped student is taking part in a shuffleboard game by using a board that has been waxed and a puck that has been waxed. He is capable of moving his arm forward, but cannot extend his hand. By placing the puck on his lap and on the edge of the board as seen above, he is able to push the puck with enough force to slide down the board.

The teacher should place the puck on the edge of the board so all the student has to do is touch it and send it sliding down the board some distance from the bottom edge of the board. Placing it in this position is the first part of the instruction. With the puck half on his lap and half on the board, the student attempts to push the puck down the board. This procedure should be in the student's realm of physical ability and should never frustrate him.

Later on in the game, the aiming responsibility can be placed with the student. Here, too, this should be geared to the student's abilities. Where possible, the student should aim the board by

Adapted shuffleboard game.

himself. This would entail moving his wheelchair from right to left with the board attached to it.

The teacher should remember to wax the puck and board prior to each class session. This permits the puck to slide further toward the high scoring numbers on the court.

The shuffleboard court can and should be modified for students such as the one in the photograph. Low numerals should be placed very close to the board and high ones a short distance away. The court should not be too narrow because the students may not be able to slide their pucks past others that have stopped close to the board. Each numeral should clearly stand out as shown in this illustration.

Several courts can be made where numerals of low value are used, such as 1, 2 and 3. Other courts can be made with numerals of higher value, such as 6, 7, 8, and 10. There are many variations of courts the teacher can make and each one will suit a particular group of students.

ICE AND ROLLER SKATING

The device appearing below was designed by this author and constructed by the pipe shop at a residential facility for the mentally and physically handicapped.

This roller skating device is constructed from pipe one quarter of an inch thick and $1\frac{1}{2}$ inches in diameter. Two pipe sections of the device are $1\frac{3}{4}$ of an inch in diameter. These are the two rounded corners of the upper rail. The lower horizontal supports are two feet long, measuring from the post, which provides a good base of support to the device. The wheels used on this piece of equipment are from a discarded hospital bed.

The device is adjustable for both height and width and can accomodate one student or two students at the same time. There is a metal bolt on each vertical post used to secure the upright firmly in place. The smaller diameter pipe has the adjusting holes in it, whereas the larger pipe has only the single fastening hole. The rail the student holds onto has an adjustment system similar to the one just mentioned. The device in the photograph is painted a bright yellow to add to the overall pleasant appearance of the equipment.

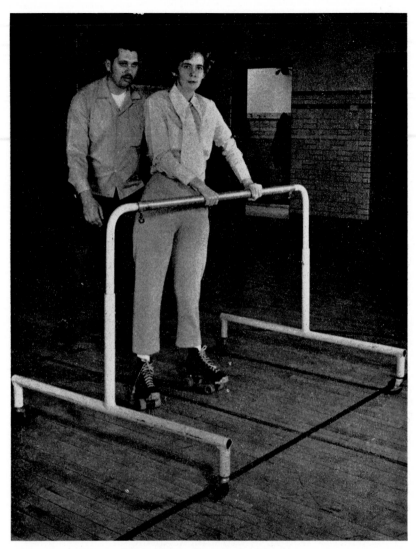

Adjustable roller skating device.

The student should receive instructions in basic skills of roller skating before he or she is ready to use the roller skating rail. Prior instructions can be given to the student with the use of some of the equipment found in the physical therapy department. Parallel bars can be used by the physical education teacher and therapist to prepare the student for the roller skating rail. Audiovisual aids should also be used for instructing the student. A loop film showing a student using the rail would be excellent in the instructional phase of the student's training.

After the student has developed some basic physical skills using various pieces of equipment in the physical therapy department, he can advance to the use of the adapted roller skating device. At first, the student should skate straight ahead, and slowly. Because the device is heavy, it will not roll away from the student but it will roll easily because of the wheels. When the student becomes more accomplished in the use of the device and in his skating ability, he can practice turning.

There should always be some competent person behind the student whenever he is using the device. This is a wise safety procedure to follow. One situation to be aware of when using this implement is the student who might fall forward and hit his chin or head on the top rail. For added safety precautions, the student should have on some type of safety belt which the spotter can grasp firmly and pull up on if the need should arise. A helmet might also be used for additional safety.

Students with mild and moderate conditions of spina bifida can use this device. To be able to use it at all, students with a moderate degree of involvement should have on long leg braces. Probably, these students will be wearing braces of some kind during school for ambulation instruction or because this was prescribed by their physicians. The severity of the student's condition will determine whether he wears short or long leg braces.

Let us consider the student with long leg braces for discussion at this time. He will have to have his braces locked at the knees and receive some support around his waist. Regular indoor roller skates can be used with this student. The teacher should be absolutely certain that the skates fit properly. As stated above, prior experience in gait training will be of value to the student when using this device. Prior training is not a prerequisite to use of this piece of equipment.

The student should be in some sort of chair in preparation for using the device. With assistance from the teacher, the student rises from his wheelchair and grasps the top rail. Once again, remember to have a spotter behind and holding onto the student. The rear wheels on the roller skating device should be locked to prevent the device from rolling away from the teacher and student. After the student is set and balanced in place, the teacher can unlock the wheels with his foot while still holding onto the student.

The device is designed so that it can be used for ice skating as well. The wheels can be easily removed and special wooden plates can be installed in their place. Solid wood should be used instead of plywood, because the latter tends to split and curl when damp. The front of the plate should curve up slightly to resemble a ski. A round wooden dowel should be permanently secured to the wooden plate. The dowel should fit firmly into the pipe opening where the wheel was housed and should be longer than the shaft of the pipe. In this way the teacher can easily grasp the dowel and remove it from the pipe.

If the teacher finds that the device is sliding too fast, a piece of sandpaper can be secured to the bottom of the plates. This would tend to keep the device from sliding too fast.

The best type of skate to use initially with the handicapped student has two blades or runners on the bottom. As each student progresses and reaches a stage which the teacher believes to be advanced, the student can attempt to use a skate with one blade. The same safety procedures should be observed for the ice skating instructions as were used for the former activity. There is one exception, however. The teacher should have on some sort of nonslip shoe or shoe covering to provide added support to himself and the student.

Both of these devices can be used in public and commercial recreational establishments. The instructor should present his program and the equipment to these two areas as was discussed in a previous section of this book. Here again, the teacher has one device that can be used for two activities for the handicapped. They would now be able to participate where they could not in the past.

SWIMMING

These special swimming devices are manufactured by the Universe Company, Altadena, California. The device should not be used to compensate for actual swimming ability of the student.

Student with muscular dystrophy using special swimming devices.

The swimming devices are only to aid the student in the course of his instruction.

The teacher has to inflate the device by blowing into a valve similar to many other plastic inflatable items. The swimming device is to be inflated after it is on the student and deflated before it is taken off. Each end of the device is fastened together by screws and bolts. This is much safer than using snaps or other means of securing the ends of the device together. Each separate device is adjustable by having several sets of holes in the ends of the device.

The student in the photograph requires the aid of six of these devices in order to practice swimming fundamentals. He receives support to three vital areas of his body. One area is his shoulders, the second is his lower back region and the third is the upper portion of his legs.

As the devices hold the student up in the water, the teacher can work with the student on moving his arms and legs in a particular swimming stroke. The devices allow the student to freely move his limbs. The instructor can also get in closer to the student to manually aid the individual in his swimming efforts. If necessary, two more of these aids can be placed under the student's chest to hold him up even further in the water.

As the student gains some proficiency with the number of devices he is using, one, two, or all of them could be taken away. The student who has muscular dystrophy will not be able to remain out of the devices long because he tires easily. The goal in using these devices is to allow the student to experience the joy of swimming and taking part in the water games with his classmates and family.

The student appearing below has extremely limited function of her lower limbs. She is able to use long-leg braces for walking, but lacks any ability to use her legs in a swimming activity.

She is able to take part in the swimming activity because of the use of the special swimming aids. At first she had to wear a swimming aid on each leg, one on each upper arm and two around her waist. Wearing these devices allowed this girl to practice her arm strokes without having her legs drag on the floor of the pool or in any other way hampering her swimming efforts.

As she developed a stronger arm stroke, the two devices secured around her waist were removed. The next step was to remove the

Student with spina bifida using special swimming devices.

devices on her arms. This was done by removing one at a time when she was ready. The photograph shows her in the next-to-last phase of her instruction. That is, there are only two devices remaining on her legs. When her skill level and self-confidence were improved, all devices were taken away. She was able to pull her body through the water and use various arm strokes in this small swimming pool pictured below.

These devices should be used in a school setting only by a highly qualified person. Such a person should be experienced in swimming and have knowledge of physical handicaps in order to conduct a swimming program.

Parents can work with their child after they have received some training from a competent physical education instructor or from a physical therapist. The parent can assist his child in the swimming activity at home when the weather permits. Geographic location will certainly have a bearing on how much time can be spent with the child at home.

Lakes, backyard swimming pools and those public swimming pools that allow the child with this condition to swim are excellent facilities for this student to take advantage of when time and weather permit.

TABLE TENNIS

The table tennis racquets appearing in the photograph above were designed by this author for those students who have difficulty in using the conventional type of racquet. These adaptations have larger striking surfaces.

The two-handled racquet at the top of the picture does not contain rubber straps. It can be used by a student who needs a larger racquet for his initial phase of instruction. Both handles on this racquet are not permanent fixtures. Either one of the handles can be removed for various students. After the student has acquired sufficient skills with his racquet, he can proceed to the use of a regulation racquet. The dimensions of this racquet are the same for the one below it.

The racquet on the bottom is $7\frac{1}{4}$ inches wide, nine inches long and three eighths of an inch thick. There is a solid wooden handle three inches long fastened to the paddle so that it extends

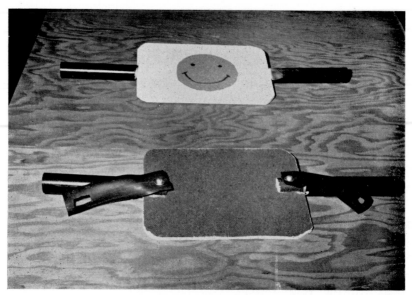

Tire innertube straps attached to a two-handled table tennis racquet.

1½ inches from the edge of the board. The section of the handle fastened to the paddle will have to be cut to conform to the flat surface of the board. The wooden handle in this case is from a broken broom handle.

The outermost handle is cut from a firm, hollow plastic tube. It is 5½ inches long and should fit firmly over the wooden handle until it touches the edge of the board. A strong glue should be used to secure the plastic handle in place.

The rubber hand grip assists are 6½ inches long and are attached by a small wood screw to the wooden handle on the back side of the paddle. These straps are 1½ inches wide with a small hole at the end which fits over the plastic handle.

The face of the racquet is covered with a piece of medium grain sandpaper which is glued in place. The striking surface can be painted or decorated in any number of ways. Painting the racquets adds a bit of color to what could be a drab looking surface.

Both racquets can be used in table tennis, tetherball or adapted target games. Many students who were unable to participate in such activities before, because of the lack of suitable devices, can

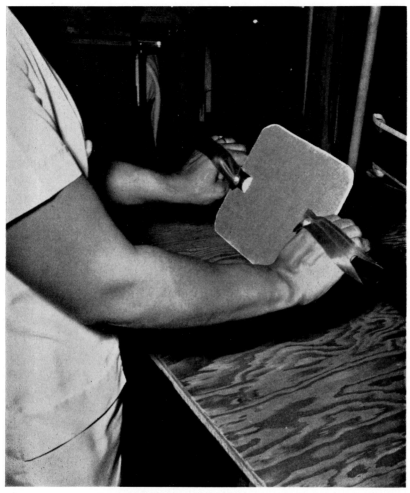

Two-handled table tennis racquet.

now find pleasure in these activities through the use of adapted equipment.

The aide in the photograph above is demonstrating the use of a two-handled table tennis racquet. This device is designed to be used by students who do not have a strong grip in either hand. These students can have various conditions such as muscular dystrophy, amyotonia congenita, other neurological conditions and arthritis, to mention a few.

The rubber straps help to hold the student's hands in place on the handle of the racquet. Even if the student was to relax his grasp or let go of the handles for whatever reason, he would still maintain his hold on the racquet because of the straps.

Each strap can be pulled toward the end of the handle to adjust to the size of the student's hands. The teacher will need to make sure the straps fit firmly over the backs of the student's hands, below his knuckles. The straps should never squeeze the student's hands too tightly, for obvious reasons.

When the student is ready to play, he or the teacher positions his hands on the handles so the top edge of the paddle is tilted slightly toward the net on the table. This way he has a better opportunity to return the ball to the table. The aide in the photograph has the racquet in the desired position. As the ball comes toward the student, he pushes the racquet forward, striking the ball, and then pulls it back to get ready for the next move. The larger striking area will give the student a greater chance of hitting the oncoming ball and returning it to the table.

This racquet can be used for table tennis as described above, and can also be used for a game of tetherball, in either a standing or seated position.

The two blind students shown below are using regulation table tennis racquets with a sponge rubber ball attached to the racquet by a string.

The string is attached to the handle of the racquet and extends from the edge of the table to eighteen inches over the net. The students are in a practice session with the instructor looking on to give each student feedback about his efforts in this activity. Having a string on each handle will allow the student to practice various strokes and serving skills at his own rate of speed.

Using this procedure, the student can practice placing the ball on the other side of the net with several kinds of strokes and a serve. When the student hits the ball, the instructor can immediately inform the student of his efforts. There will be those times when the instructor will have to be at another teaching station and students will still need to know of their efforts. Several bells can be tied to the top of the net so they hang down approximately one inch. Each student takes a turn practicing with this special racquet

Blind students using individual practice table tennis racquets.

so there will be no doubt when the ball is hit over or into the net. If the ball hits the net before it goes over it, the bells will ring. Even though there is no feed-back from the instructor, the bells inform the student immediately if he hit the ball high enough to go over the net.

The next phase of instruction for these two students is to use the broom handle standard with the sponge rubber ball attached to it. Here, each student takes one turn at hitting the ball with one of the several strokes he was practicing with the ball and string. He can also practice serving as well. When each student is ready for a game, the sponge rubber ball is changed for a hollow plastic practice ball the size of a softball with a bell inside of it. A ball this size certainly gives the blind student a larger target to hit and a better chance to hit it. As each student develops greater skill in serving and returning the ball, a smaller hollow plastic practice ball the size of a golf ball can be brought into play. This is done on an individual student basis.

Rules of the game and scoring procedures can be established

by each instructor for his particular students. What must be remembered, however, is that the students—all of them—should be able to score points in whatever system the teacher has developed. This does not mean that each student should win a game each time he plays, but that his individual skills should relate to the scoring criteria. An example of a scoring system this author has used for blind and partially sighted students is as follows. One point for a successful serve, two points for a return that did not go over the net and three points for a return that did go over the net; in this way the student is not penalized for missing a return over the net, but is rewarded for his efforts. Certainly other systems will be devised by other instructors, which is this author's hope, and more blind and partially sighted students will be able to participate in the table tennis activity.

The standard seen in the photograph below is constructed from broken and discarded broom handles. Many devices can be constructed from broom handles or the handles can be added to existing devices to make them suitable for certain handicapped individuals to use as discussed in other sections of this chapter.

The standard pictured below is seventy-five inches high, with a cement base which is eight inches in diameter. There are three inches of cement in the circular base. Ready-mix cement was prepared and poured into a large metal can. The lower section of the standard should be suspended from some sort of overhang into the middle of the base while the cement is hardening.

The top horizontal extension is twenty inches long measuring from the verticle upright. The top section of the standard can be raised seven inches when a larger ball is used or when the instructor does not want the ball to touch the table surface. The height adjustment can also benefit the game of tetherball for those individuals seated in wheelchairs.

The two sections fit together because each of them has a right-angle groove cut into it, as shown in the photograph. The length of the grooves will depend on how high the teacher wishes the standard to be. Four holes, each one quarter of an inch in diameter, can be drilled in each section of the standard. Two metal bolts with butterfly fasteners should be used to secure the sections together. Using this type of fastener will eliminate the need for

Adjustable broom handle standard with cement base

hand tools each time the standard is adjusted. The teacher can use his hand to tighten the bolts enough for the sections to remain firmly togther.

The teacher will find many more uses for the adjustable broom handle standard in his recreation or physical education program. Much smaller versions can be made for table use, incorporating the same means of construction.

VOLLEYBALL

Volleyball game.

The students in this class are using a large, lightweight ball that has been discussed previously in this chapter. The ball is larger than a regulation size volleyball, but not larger than a regulation size high school basketball.

Certain rules of the game had to be modified to meet the needs of each student. For one, the size and weight of the ball were changed and another was that the net was lowered. This way, those students who could not hit the ball over a high net could succeed with the lowered one. The boundary lines were also changed in the back of the playing area of each side. This brought the students a little closer so each of them would have a chance at hitting the ball.

The scoring system this author used was that every ball which was hit over the net, except the serve, was worth two points. Each ball that was hit forward was worth one point. The ball could even be hit toward the net, falling to the floor, and still be worth one point. The idea behind this scoring system was to give each student a chance to score points for his team.

Those students who could not serve the ball over the net from any close position on the court could use another method. The student would serve the ball to a fellow teammate and he in turn had to pass the ball over the net in one motion. This way, the first student did, in effect, serve the ball.

This same playing and serving procedure was used with large beach balls and balloons. All three of these playing implements proved to be enjoyable and successful for all the students involved in the unit, regardless of the severity of their condition.

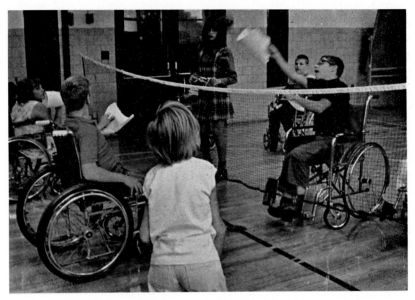

Net scoopball game.

The scoops being used in this game were made from plastic bleach bottles. A scoop can be made by positioning the bottle on a table with the handle facing toward you. Find the base of the handle and measure horizontally two inches to the right and cut straight down to the bottom. Do the same thing on the left side. Now begin to remove this section by cutting from the upper corner of the first cut over to the upper corner of the second cut. Next, measure up one inch from the bottom of the bottle and cut all the way around the bottom. At this point, you should have a scoop. Make sure to discard the scrap piece of plastic. All that remains is to round the corners off and trim all the edges so they are smooth. Keep the cap on the scoop because you might want to use this device for some sort of water game, either in the swimming pool or in an outdoor activity.

This author has used the scoop in games such as scoop volleyball which is seen above. It has also been used in scoop baseball, scoop bowling and target games using the scoop to propel objects. Of course, special rules and procedures were used in each game for various students, depending on their type and degree of handicap.

On many occasions the students cut their own scoops in the physical education setting. Those who could not use a conventional pair of scissors used specially designed ones that had more than two finger placement holes in them. After they cut the scoops, the teacher should check to make sure the edges are safe and not jagged. Many students decorated their scoops, making their own designs. Felt-tip markers, crayons and watercolor paints were used by some of the students. Other articles were used as well, such as pictures from sports magazines. The students cut out portions or whole pictures from magazines and pasted them on their scoops. This can be an enjoyable activity as well as an educational one.

Presented here were a few methods of utilizing scoops in the adapted physical education program and the recreation program as well. Many variations to each activity mentioned here can be devised by the teacher for his particular group of students. The emphasis with this piece of equipment is that it can very easily be made in the home by the student or with parental assistance. This is one way of involving the family as a whole in an enjoyable and inexpensive activity.

SAFETY

Every physical education program, including the facility, must be programmed to eliminate the possibility of accidents or injuries to students and staff. Each instructor should be aware of areas where accidents are likely to occur. Some of these areas are faulty physical education devices, poor play area facilities, personal physical conditions of students and the unexpected. This chapter will attempt to inform the reader about the variety of safety aspects to be aware of when working with the handicapped students.

IN AND OUT OF THE SCHOOL PLANT

It is the responsibility of the teacher to inspect the physical education setting, both indoors and out, prior to any instruction. There should be an adequate fire escape route which a physically handicapped student can use in case of such an emergency. This ruling is set by the local fire department and state authorities.

Lighting, heating and ventilation are included in the discussion on safety because they influence the educational atmosphere and the well-being of the student. All rooms used for physical education should be well lighted, especially for those students who are partially sighted. The need for adequate heat and ventilation is obvious.

If there are devices or structures that protrude into or onto the playing area, they should be removed if possible. When working in an area containing an obstacle or equipment that cannot be removed or avoided, then sound safety rules must be established. Students should be made aware of these rules prior to the use of this area (Kirchner, 1966). If, for any reason, the obstacles cannot be removed, suitable safety precautions should be taken. One method that can employed is to place shock-absorbing padding around protruding objects. Pulleys can be used to raise and lower certain devices when needed.

All water fountains should be recessed into the wall along with faucet handles. It would be practical to install two separate water fountains. One would be for those students in wheelchairs and one for those who are able to walk. Many times it is difficult for a student in a whelchair to get a drink from a water fountain that is too high for him to reach and injuries have occurred.

An elevator should be available in a school where physically handicapped students are in attendance. This would permit easy accessibility to the gymnasium. Carrying students up and down stairs increases the probability of an accident with possible injury to student and/or teacher. A practice of this nature should be discouraged and other more suitable arrangements made. It would be best if the physically handicapped could occupy rooms on the first floor of the school building.

Most schools have some sort of outdoor play area. The play areas are usually made of concrete, asphalt, grass, sand or a combination of each. For the sake of clarity, swings, slides and the usual playground equipment will not be discussed when referring to safety on the playground or play area. The emphasis here is on adapted physical education equipment.

The teacher must be aware of large cracks or holes in the concrete and any protrusions from the surface. Under no circumstances should students be playing close to doors that open out, or stairways leading down to the gymnasium or entrance to the building.

The preceding were safety precautions pertaining to structural facilities. Each school will have varied play area formations and terrains. The terrain of the school will allow some activities and make others impossible. Consideration of this and other factors discussed should be planned for prior to conducting physical education activities outdoors. There are other safety precautions to be taken when instructing mentally and physically handicapped students. In the following sections of this chapter, certain areas will be discussed in relation to equipment, students, medical conditions and others.

CARE OF EQUIPMENT BEFORE AND AFTER USE

Caring for equipment should become a routine procedure. Each teacher should evaluate his present inventory of equipment. Repairs should be made to those devices that can be used safely after being repaired. Unsafe equipment should be discarded and new items constructed or ordered as replacements. There should always be several extra pieces of equipment for any one class rather than just enough for each student. This, of course, applies to those pieces of equipment used by a majority of the students, and not the one-of-a-kind devices. When ordering or making equipment, always keep this point in mind.

Prior to each new unit of instruction, all devices should be examined for broken, loose or missing parts. If the piece of equipment needs to be repainted, then this is an item to be placed on a list of things to do, along with other major and minor repairs. These repairs should be made as soon as possible to prevent a long delay and inactivity for the student.

Cleaning the equipment as prescribed by some commercial manufacturers will prolong the life of the material or device. Fait (1966) mentions that cleaning the equipment will also lessen the chance of infection for a student who is susceptible to infection, such as a diabetic. When it is a teacher-made device, the teacher is best aware of how to clean and care for it.

The care of electrical devices used in various units of instruction is extremely important. Those devices mentioned in the section on storage will usually have a cabinet reserved for them. Making sure the storage area is free from moisture will also prolong the life of the equipment (Daughtrey, 1967). These pieces of equipment also need to be examined for worn out parts and minor damage. Burned-out tubes or bulbs will occur when the device is in use; therefore, spare tubes and projector bulbs need to be kept on hand.

Records that are badly scratched or cracked will need to be replaced. The teacher should have at least two of the same type of records in his collection. An example of this would be two square dance records of similar type and tempo.

Devices used by students require routine inspection. Wheelchairs, wheelchair ramps, crutches and other mechanical aids need to be checked and cared for. There will be times when repairs must be made right away. The person performing the repairs must have a basic knowledge of the device if he is going to repair it properly. Whenever the student is able, he should perform the inspection of his ambulation aids and report any repairs that need to be made to his teacher or therapist. This is one of the responsibilities the student should be aware of in the physical education setting.

When returning the adapted devices to the storage areas, the teacher will want to check for newly damaged, loosened or missing parts. This he can do quickly as the apparatus is being replaced in the storage compartments.

Nets used for all net games need to be examined for worn-out strands. The longer these are allowed to go without repair, the more strain will be placed on the other sections of the net, causing additional damage. Frayed strands need to be repaired before the next use if the life of the equipment is to be extended.

These are but a few of the recommendations for the care of physical education equipment. If the teacher establishes a constant routine of equipment management and safety checks, he can always count on having devices for his present students and those in the future.

MEDICAL EVALUATION

Certain physical handicaps need special attention with respect to medical evaluation or directives set by the student's physician. Before any actual instruction, the teacher should comprehend the medical diagnosis of each member of his class. The instructor will gain much of the pertinent information from the student's medical record. It is a wise practice to consult with the student's physician before introducing the student to a new unit. Oftentimes, there are standard forms used by schools, stating the child's medical condition, what physical activities he can and cannot participate in and any limiting factors in those in which he can participate.

An adapted physical education activity form such as the one above can be of great assistance to the teacher when planning for an individualized program of activities for a handicapped student.

BATTLE CREEK PUBLIC SCHOOLS
Division of Instruction
Department of Health and Physical Education

ADAPTIVE PHYSICAL EDUCATION ACTIVITY GUIDE

Pupil_____ Date_____

School_____

Adaptive Physical Education Teacher_____

Check any of the following that should be omitted:

MOVEMENTS

Bending ( )	Kicking ( )	Running ( )
Climbing ( )	Lifting ( )	Stretching ( )
Hanging ( )	Pulling ( )	Throwing ( )
Jumping ( )	Pushing ( )	Twisting ( )

Please check (x) either generally or individually the types of Physical Education which you recommend for this pupil.

Strenuous ( )	*Moderate ( )*	*Mild ( )*
____Basketball	____Running and Walking	____Badminton Practice
____Calisthenics	____Shooting Baskets	____Corrective Exercises
____Hand Ball	____Swimming	____Free Throwing
____Rope Climbing	(Non-competitive)	____Horseshoes
____Running Half Mile	____Table Tennis	____Playing Catch
____Soccer	____Touch Football	____Swimming (Recreational)
____Swim. (Competitive)	____Volley Ball	____Archery
____Tumbling-Gymnastics		____Bowling
____Wrestling		

Suggested corrective exercises or activities.

Adapted Physical Education for period of_____19__ to _____19__.

Signature of Physician_____

Adapted physical education activity form.
(Form courtesy Battle Creek Public Schools, Battle Creek, Michigan)

These directions are to be followed to insure the safety of the student and the professional well-being of the instructor. Written permission forms should be obtained for any activity which does not appear on the form.

Instructors would also gain much from consulting with the physical and occupational therapist with whom the student is working. These people can give the teachers insight into how the individual performs in their respective settings. Both of these adjunctive services will be able to provide the teacher with correct techniques used in certain physical maneuvers with the physically handicapped individual. They can also recommend the use and type of protective equipment where it is indicated by the physician. They can be very helpful by aiding the teacher in designing and building adapted physical education equipment especially suited for a certain student.

There are several phyiscal conditions that require special safety precautions. One of these is muscular dystrophy. Here, any attempt to lift a student from underneath the shoulder area could cause a dislocation of one or both shoulders. The student should avoid long, hard and resistive physical activities; that is, allow the student to take part, but not to the point of being fatigued.

Sensory loss to the student with spina bifida must be uppermost in the mind of the instructor when working with this student. The student's lower limbs should be covered with long leg trousers when he is participating in an activity in which his legs will come in contact with the floor, tumbling mats or pieces of equipment. This will help prevent skin abrasions to the student's legs.

This author holds that all students should be allowed to develop whatever physical skills they have and acquire new ones in a planned and structured setting. In all instances, trained personnel can make the difference between injury and enjoyment. When a trained person is present, the student who is known to have seizures, for example, will have a responsible individual to rely upon should the need ever arise. It is, of course, solely up to the physician to decide what physical activities the student can take part in and to what degree. Personal efforts, self-image, home environment, school life and previous training are factors which will determine the difference in the rate of accomplishment by the student.

PROPER CLOTHING

For certain units of instruction, loose-fitting clothing is best. It affords the student a freer range of movement and the teacher a better chance of aiding the student. A stretch fabric is best for most physical activities. In some instances, various students may wish to wear certain clothing to cover a skin condition (Fait, 1966). This would also be a good procedure to protect a wound which is healing. The student's wishes should certainly be granted and special considerations should be made in all of the physical activities. Some items of clothing might be prescribed by the student's physician for added protection.

It would be a time-saving and practical technique to install zippers on the lower, outer portion of the pant leg for those students who wear long or short leg braces. This will permit freedom of movement and an easy on and off procedure for shoes and braces. Parents will find that they may have to purchase larger-sized trousers to accomodate the addition of the braces.

Students susceptible to respiratory infections would have to wear clothing for a longer period of time, perhaps well into warm weather. When others are wearing lightweight coats, these students would have to wear heavier coats. This would also apply to students with muscular dystrophy, amyotonia congenita and those with respiratory conditions.

When going outdoors for activities, it would be wise to require that those students who are prone to falls wear a safe protective headgear. This safety procedure could also apply indoors.

There are those, including this author, who do advocate swimming for the spina bifida. Many health boards do not allow these students in public pools because of their bowel and bladder incontinence. It has been demonstrated that these indivduals can enter swimming pools after the proper precautions have been taken. This technique has already been discussed in Chapter One in the section on spina bifida. Newman (1970) has had success with her swimming program for the spina bifida student. She states that if safety and health precautions are taken, many of the spina bifida can learn to swim.

SUPERVISION

Supervision for the adapted physical education program is usually handled by a master teacher or a department head. When a single school is involved, the master teacher is responsible for the organization and planning of the program. When on a school district basis, the responsibility belongs to the department head or a physical education consultant. Whatever the scheme, immediate supervision is the responsibility of the individual teacher instructing the class.

It is the master teacher's duty to instruct the non and semi-trained personnel in the various techniques used in the instruction of handicapped students. The use of equipment and adapting the devices to the mentally and physically handicapped student is of primary importance. Safety habits and proper attitudes toward the student are also of concern to the helpers in the class. The supervising teacher must always be aware of the aide who is developing inappropriate habits. Inaccurate directions or responses can damage the student's learning experience, enjoyment and even his own self image. If the directions on how to use an adapted device are incorrect, then the student will not be able to use the device as it was designed.

The helper needs to know what the adapted device is to do for a particular student. Two important aspects of the safe use of equipment are (a) how is the student to use the device and (b) where must the aide assist him? Supervisors should always encourage any helper to bring forward any new or modified devices that he might have in mind which would benefit any of the students. In this way, the aides will be made to feel that they too have something to offer the student and program.

Supervision for field trips, contests and sporting events has already been discussed in other chapters.

PROGRAMMING TO ELIMINATE ACCIDENTS

Programming to eliminate accidents is an important part of teaching physical education and requires constant safety awareness. Lesson plans and unit plans will not be discussed as they pertain to the actual teaching. Rather, emphasis is placed on the safety aspect of the facility, equipment and staff as they relate to the instruction.

Every piece of equipment must be inspected prior to student use. Wooden objects need to be looked at for rough edges or splinters that can cause injuries. Any device that will support the student's weight should be carefully inspected, as should any device that has moving parts.

The system of obtaining and returning equipment must also be planned so accidents will not be caused. Students who are receiving equipment from the storage area should do so from one side and depart from the other. For example, students obtaining shuffleboard equipment from a storage closet should come from the right and leave from the left. This would cut down on the chance of crowding and rushing for equipment. The same procedure is best when returning equipment. If the students are allowed to obtain the equipment themselves, then the devices need to be stored or placed so the students do not need to climb on a stepladder to get them or move heavy objects out of the way.

A simple rule to follow for the student in a wheelchair is that the device being obtained should not be higher than the tallest person seated in the wheelchair can reach. These students should be instructed in the proper way to transport a device from the storage area to the assigned teaching station. Not only are the above safety aspects important, but the teacher should consider every facet on the watch for possible accidents. Irwin (1951) also comments on some important safety features in the physical education setting that are to be considered prior to and during instruction. When leaving and returning from the gymnasium, hallways should be clear of equipment and protruding objects.

One other area of programming needs to be discussed and that is the planning of the indoor and outdoor facilities. The adapted physical education instructor must plan with other personnel using the same area at the same time. He would need to know the number of students using the area and the activity being conducted (Irwin 1951). There are those times where two and even three groups will have to share the same activity area. When physically handicapped students are included in this situation, the above statements are important to the safety of the students.

Accidents need not occur if all staff members are aware of how the equipment is to be used in the setting for which it was designed.

The students, too, are to be responsible for their actions to the degree that they are able. The teacher in charge must carefully train his aides, students and himself to plan for the expected and unexpected, which could mean injury to any of these people. An injury can bring an enjoyable experience to a quick close. Even if the injury is minor, it can cause some of the students to become frightened of the activity. Worst of all, the student can lose confidence in the instructor. Being safety-minded is a full time responsibility.

TRANSPORTATION

T RANSPORTATION FOR THE physically handicapped can be provided in three basic modes, these being the station wagon, van or school bus. The size of the class, including teacher and helpers, will generally determine which of these vehicles will be used. The following sections will attempt to demonstrate the need for special equipment in areas of transportation and related devices.

STAFF

Whenever possible, the driver of the vehicle should not be the sole supervising individual. There should always be at least two other responsible persons in the veihcle to act as aides or helpers. If there are female students on the trip, then one of the aides would have to be a reliable adult female. A good ratio for students and aides is one aide per five students. This ratio is recommended for ambulatory students who do not require the use of additional ambulation aids. It would be best if one of the aides was responsible for any physical education equipment taken along on a trip.

When more severely handicapped students are in one of the vehicles, the aide to student ratio changes. There would need to be one aide to every handicapped student who could not move his own wheelchair or who exhibited extreme difficulty in doing so. These aides are sometimes referred to as "pushers." This aide's duty on a field trip, for example, is to help the student move through, around and over obstacles he could not handle unassisted. Even where a student can operate his wheelchair, an aide would still have to assist in situations which are unfamiliar to the student. Sometimes there is a need for aides when time is a major factor.

All staff members need to be aware of the proper methods of navigation for a student in a wheelchair who encounters curbs, steps and ramps. This will insure the safety of the student. Seat belts should always be worn by the student, regardless of his proficiency with a wheelchair. On some occasions, protective helmets are to be used for maximum student safety. Only those persons who are qualified and trained should do any of the bodily lifting of a handicapped student. This applies to the safety of the student and person doing the lifting. Various staff members should be familiarized in the use of special devices on certain vehicles. The next section will discuss the special equipment unique to the transportation of handicapped persons.

SPECIAL EQUIPMENT AND VEHICLES

There are various devices available for the transportation of physically handicapped students. These devices are in the form of additions to building sites and vehicles.

A device which is very valuable in the transportation of the handicapped is a portable wooden wheelchair ramp. The ramp would also benefit those students who use crutches. Plywood, three quarters of an inch thick, is suitable for this purpose. The surface of the ramp should be covered with a weather-resistant paint. While the paint is still wet, a light coat of sand should be spread over the surface of the ramp. This author believes this type of ramp covering is better than a rubber runner or strips of a nonslip material on the ramp. When the paint dries, the sand will securely adhere to the surface of the ramp, making it slip-proof, especially in wet weather. The traction on this ramp is extremely good. The height of the ramp should be the approximate height of an average curb.

Even though many new school buildings are constructed on one level, there are still curbs leading to the building. Entrances and exits should have ramps for the students in wheelchairs or those on crutches. Stationary ramps are especially needed for the exit that leads to the playing field. These ramps should be made of concrete because they will remain outdoors permanently. The State of Michigan (1966) makes provisions for special building facilities for those who are handicapped. These provisions state that the minimum length for a stationary ramp is five feet. A width of three feet is minimum if used only by those in wheelchairs and six feet if used by all pedestrian traffic (State of Michigan, 1966). A handrail is to be installed on both sides of the ramp for added safety and accessibility by the handicapped.

Another device used for transporting handicapped persons is a hydraulic hoist. The hoist is on wheels so it can be rolled from the student's classroom to a vehicle. A sling type seat fits around the student's lower back and buttocks and should be under him while he is still sitting in the wheelchair. The teacher raises the student up and pushes him toward the waiting vehicle. The process is reversed when lowering the student into his seat in the vehicle. This is the safest means of lifting the student from his wheelchair into a bus or into a van.

It is safer and easier to embark and disembark students from a bus that has a hydraulic side lift as the one in the photograph below.

Here the student is being lowered to the ground in his wheel-

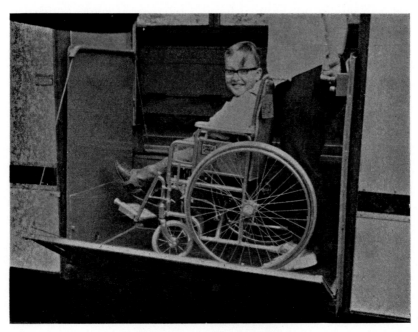

Bus with a wheelchair lift.

chair. This type of lift is the safest and quickest means of transportation available for the handicapped student. The student does not have to leave his own chair throughout the duration of a trip. The bus is equipped with special devices that hold the wheelchair to the floor. Each student is wheeled onto the platform, his wheelchair brakes are applied and then he is raised into the bus by an aide. The part of the lift that is the ramp when the lift is down, becomes the gate when the lift is raised or lowered. This safeguard would prevent the student's chair from accidentally rolling off the lift. The lift would also be ideal for the student who must rely on the use of crutches. Many bus steps are too narrow and high for this student.

There will be instances when the bus with the lift cannot be used. Other alternatives open to the teacher are the use of a station wagon or an enclosed van. Whichever one is used, one problem arises. That problem is the storage space for the wheelchairs. Collapsible wheelchairs are best in an instance such as this. Unless the floor in a van is equipped to secure students in wheelchairs, the van should not be used for this purpose. It could be used to haul the wheelchairs and the station wagon could carry the students.

The teacher will have to investigate his school's surroundings for areas that are in need of special modifications or additions. A curb that is a little too high for wheelchairs, lavatory facilities, locker room accomodations and other items will have to be modified for the handicapped student.

If the handicapped student is unable to safely go from the school site to other educational and recreational areas, then those concerned with transportation will have to consider some modifications in this area. It is not an ideal setting where a student in a wheelchair or one on crutches cannot take advantage of an activity just because of the limitations placed on him by the facility.

••••••••••••••••••••••••••• **CHAPTER 7** •••••••••••••••••••••••••••

ENVIRONMENTAL INFLUENCES

Many times the area being used for adapted physical education will facilitate or hamper the program. Oftentimes, the size, shape, contour and construction can affect the educational process.

PHYSICAL PLANT

In many cases the gymnasium is the facility or area which is used most of the time for physical education activities. There are some instances where special rooms are used for certain adapted exercises. These rooms contain specialized pieces of equipment designed to correct or strengthen an injured part of the body. An example would be a weight training room, or a table games room. These types of rooms will not be discussed here, but rather the physical plant in general.

The entrance and exit doorways should have double doors without a center post. It would be best if there were no riser of any kind in the threshold to make entering and leaving unsafe and difficult for those on crutches or in wheelchairs. These two items can allow freedom of movement, or can restrict the handicapped student from using an educational setting.

Door handles can be placed lower so that a student in a wheelchair can open the door by himself. A piece of Velcro material could be placed around the knob, making it easier for a handicapped student to grip the handle. If the door has a panic bar on it, then it too can be placed slightly lower to allow the student in the wheelchair to open the door by himself. All of these modifications should be planned in advance or be made as the need arises.

Floor manufacturers have developed a more resilient floor surface which is designed to reduce the number of serious accidents. The floor actually absorbs the shock of an object falling on it. This

141

type of surface would benefit the normal student as well as the physically handicapped one.

The physical plant also applies to the outdoor activity area. There are certain sports activities that need to be conducted on a grass or clay surface. Students in wheelchairs may find it difficult to move on grass, thereby reducing the types of activities the student can take part in. This author believes the clay surface to be the ideal playing surface. Here, all the students can freely move about without becoming too fatigued. The decreased resistance to their wheelchairs or crutches makes this possible. On other surfaces such as asphalt or concrete, the student can move about in his wheelchair or crutches with ease, but would sustain a more serious injury if he should fall.

The physical education building, wing or room should provide easy accessibility to the student. Certain situations might arise when special adaptations need to be made to the school structure. Such adaptations could include a concrete ramp from a curb, a sidewalk to the play area and the installation of a double doorway.

COMMERCIAL RECREATIONAL ESTABLISHMENTS

Commercial recreational establishments constructed within the last fifteen years were designed to be roomy, well lighted and free from many inside obstacles. Steps leading into these establishments have almost been eliminated from the modern recreational site. The modern, one-floor establishment has provided additional recreational areas for the handicapped.

Bowling establishments that are on the ground level conform to the ideal setting for the person in a wheelchair. Miniature golf courses have adequate space for wheelchairs in and around their settings. Roller skating and ice skating facilities are also being built with the one-floor concept in mind. The movable skating support which appeared in Chapter Four would be of great value in these last two facilities. Architects are planning for the most efficient type of building which would suit all persons using it. This idea will certainly benefit the physically handicapped individual.

Owners and managers of these establishments are becoming more aware of the needs of handicapped patrons by permitting the use of specialized pieces of equipment in their facilities. Special bowling leagues are being developed and expanded for the retarded, physically handicapped and those who are blind. This could not be if it were not for the cooperation and understanding of the owners of these bowling establishments.

The responsibility the teacher has to the owners of these recreational establishments is to make certain the equipment is safe and that it in no way harms the owners' property. This author has found that, in most cases, owners are willing to retain one or two devices in their buildings for use by the handicapped patrons. The handicapped can then use the adapted devices at any time.

The teacher and the owner of the recreational establishment can work together to increase the amount of time the handicapped can participate in activities at this site. Special school events can also be held at these facilities, such as a class field trip, school competition or parent-child bowling day. These are just a few examples of how the commercial recreational establishment can be utilized.

PUBLIC RECREATIONAL ESTABLISHMENTS

Public recreational establisments are usually administered on a city or county basis. When considering the influence the public recreation department could have on the handicapped, one must take into account two points of view. One view, held by some, is that the handicapped should be included in any activity they enjoy. This would mean the handicapped person would be involved in any activity the recreation program had to offer. The other view is that a special program of recreational activities should be developed for these people (Daniels, 1954).

Certainly, whatever the case, the adapted physical education teacher should work with the recreation personnel to make their facilities available to his students. After the handicapped student leaves the school program, he needs to have a place he can use for his leisure time. For example, such places could be the ones already mentioned, such as an archery range or a family-type billiard establishment. The commercial facilities are adequate, but they are restrictive in what they are intended for; this person needs a wide variety of activities, as any normal individual does for leisure time enjoyment.

The recreation department can broaden its influence in the community by having activities for the handicapped. This should be on an all-year basis, with the out-of-school months being the most active. Adapted equipment can be made by the recreation personnel and stored in their departments. This will enable the handicapped to come and be part of a group which is involved in recreational activities. Socialization becomes a positive avenue of growth for these people.

SEASONS

This section is, of course, relative to the geographic location in which the teacher is working. A teacher in the northern section of the United States, for example, will have some additional physical activities that a teacher in a year-round warm climate would not have.

Weather conditions or seasons determine the type of equipment needed, storage space, transportation and physical plant. Colder areas will require more indoor activities than will warmer areas. Irwin (1951) stresses the consideration of climate conditions when planning for indoor space. Additional activity areas would be ideal in a cold climate. This would permit more students to have added space for their activities. Those in warm or mild areas can make use of outdoor facilities for a longer period of time.

Adaptations to certain pieces of equipment will need to be made in cold areas. Sleds will have to be modified to meet the safety needs of a handicapped student. Ice skates will also have to be modified so the handicapped student can participate in this activity. This does not mean that the teacher in the warmer climate should totally ignore winter sports; he should present such sports for discussion at least. There are western and southern states that do have a snowfall. Even though it may last for only a short time, the teacher can take advantage of an additional source of learning and enjoyment.

Snow sleds can be adapted for the handicapped by constructing a guide line for the sled. A steel pole should be driven into the top and bottom of a gentle slope. A strong, taught rope should be secured between the poles. The sled itself can be adapted by placing spring-loaded clips under the sled in the front and in the rear. The sled is then attached to the rope by means of the clips. Hand grips could be placed on the sled for those students who need them. Two, and possibly three, safety belts should go around the student when he is on the sled. These safety belts should be secured to the sled. Maintaining the tautness of the rope will ensure that the sled does not veer off course. A long sled is best to use because it will keep the student's legs from dragging in the snow. After the sled has gone down the course, the teacher can remove it from the guide rope and carry it back to the start for the next student.

Many commercial recreational establishments will not have or purchase specialized pieces of equipment. The instructor can donate a piece of adapted equipment and assure the proprietor of the benefits of having a safe device in his establishment. This is just a beginning to the full integration of the handicapped into the scheme of the community.

These are but a few of the influences the above mentioned settings and conditions have on the types of adapted physical education equipment that will be used. It is the responsibility of the teacher to have his students exposed to the advantages of these settings.

AUDIOVISUAL AIDS

IN ADDITION TO THE use of adapted physical education equipment, audiovisual aids are a superb means of educating handicapped students. Graton (1964) points out in her book that the mentally retarded will learn more quickly with the use of audiovisual devices than from teacher explanations. These students are best taught when they can see, hear or use the object in discussion. This author believes this same premise to be true for the physically handicapped student as well.

The kinds of audiovisual aids which will be discussed in this chapter should be varied in their uses by the teacher. There are numerous ways and combinations in which these aids can be utilized. The extent to which they are used will rest with each teacher.

Audiovisual materials are extremely valuable to any instructional unit. Each teacher must consider the capabilities of his students for using any of the devices he places at their disposal. Both physical and emotional capabilities are items which will determine if a student may use one or all of the materials. Students who are physically handicapped may only be able to operate a few of the devices, but they should be made to feel that they are still capable of learning to use other audiovisual aids.

One factor which could determine the use of many audiovisual aids is whether or not the activities are presented out-of-doors. It is very difficult to take a movie or film strip projector outside, but a portable tape recorder and bulletin boards are definite possibilities. Under certain circumstances, a portable record player could be used.

The following sections will describe various audiovisual aids and how they can be used in the adapted physical education program together with the adapted equipment.

BULLETIN BOARDS

The material on the bulletin board should be kept simple—not overcrowded, colorful, and appealing to the students. It is very important to keep the items on the board at a moderate number. If too many pictures are used, the students will tend to disregard the bulletin board entirely. Items on the board should be changed frequently so the students do not become used to them. The initial purpose of the bulletin board is to develop an interest in the activity.

Pictures should be clear and express the theme of the unit. Abstract designs or explanations are to be avoided for the mentally retarded and physically handicapped student. It is best to have large pictures that can be plainly seen from a nearby section of the gymnasium. In this way, the teacher can exhibit the items on the bulletin board to all at one time.

When titles are used the letters should stand out, but not confuse the students. The teacher will find it best to use letters of the same color in the titles. Titles would be best placed on the same plane to make it easier for the child who has difficulty reading.

There should be a balance of materials on the bulletin board. The teacher can accomplish this by providing space on the class board for the students' work as well as the teacher's materials. The students can also have a bulletin board of their own. This board would still have to follow the general rules for the use of such an aid. In the physical education setting, each student can prepare a bulletin board on a specific activity he has taken part in, showing drawings and photographs. These two media can show the student using adapted devices for each segment of the unit. Bulletin board assignments can be on a rotating schedule. Several students can use the boards for one school week, and the next week a different set of students can take their turn.

Placement of the permanent bulletin board is of importance in the make-up of the gymnasium or play room. First, the students must be able to view the board at eye level or nearly eye level.

The author is considering the student's eye level. This would include the student in the wheelchair as well. Second, the bulletin board should not be placed where it will either interfere with an activity or where it will be struck by equipment during the course of the activity. Last, the bulletin board should be in a conspicious place where all can see it. The physical facility will largely determine where the bulletin board will be placed. Windows, doorways, hanging equipment and some types of lighting will restrict the placement of the bulletin board.

The following are various types or means of exhibiting materials in the physical education class. Easels, room dividers, screens, felt boards, pegboards and permanent bulletin boards are types of bulletin boards used by many teachers. One, or any number of these, can be used for a single unit of instruction. The types used will depend on the physical activity area and the unit of instruction.

Since the bulletin board is used to enhance the unit of instruction, it should show a variety of materials during each separate unit. Sports action color photographs, student-made drawings and teacher-made crafts are items that can be placed on one of the various bulletin boards used throughout the year. Snapshots taken at a field trip, show, demonstration, sporting event or at a competition should also be used on the bulletin board at various times. It is highly recommended that the teacher continue to add to his supply of colorful sport and recreation action photographs. Collecting discarded sports and recreation magazines should be a pastime of the physical education and classroom teachers.

Bulletin boards can be used to mount records of individual students or the class as a whole. For example, physical fitness data can be charted and then placed on the class bulletin board. Another example is a list of physical skills the students are to attempt to learn. This can also be charted in a form suitable to the teacher and then placed on the class bulletin board. A small bulletin board can be used to store the students' personal progression or skill cards. This small board can have horizontal slats attached to the board and dividers for each class or student, depending on the size of each class in the program. In this way, the student has a place to keep his record card where it can always be found.

Bulletin boards should be made from material that will permit the use of thumb tacks, staples or pins. Cork is a very good material which will hold these fasteners and not show holes when they are properly removed. Paint, or different colors of burlap, can be used to cover the cork material. Framing the bulletin board gives it a finished and neat appearance.

One exciting bulletin board would be that depicting mechanical action taking place. Small electrical motors, powered by batteries, are very good for this purpose. The ingenious teacher can make life-like figures with gears and levers, simulating a certain physical skill. This would certainly create interest in the bulletin board and the material on it. A bulletin board such as this one would be good to present to the students at the start of a unit.

The reader should use the ideas presented here and suit them to his own physical environment, needs and students.

CAMERAS AND PROJECTORS

Cameras and projectors have an important place in the adapted physical education program. Both of these devices have a role in the ideal educational program.

The eight millimeter motion picture camera, the Polaroid Land® cameras and cameras designed to take slides are needed implements in the teacher's supply of equipment. The eight millimeter motion picture camera is for teacher and selected student use. A good motion picture camera to have is one with a reliable photoelectric cell which makes the exposure of the lens entirely automatic. A camera with a zoom lens is preferred here, because the teacher can change from one lens magnification to another with ease. Magazine loading cameras are easier to load than spool-type cameras. The chance of exposing the film by accident is almost impossible with the magazine type.

Motion pictures can be used to take pictorial records of students and their efforts in a certain physical education activity. These films can be shown to a therapist, family and other teachers. Another use of the motion picture camera is student-made movies. Students can put together a small, or an extensive, exhibition as a class project. One student can be assigned to use the camera by the teacher while the other students assume the remaining responsibilities in making of the film. The teacher must make sure the student taking the movies is familiarized with the use of the camera.

A class-made film can be a project for each class in the program capable of undertaking such a venture. Some of the classes involved will not be as elaborate as others but the idea of making the film is the important thing.

A self, or automatic threading projector is best for the physical education setting; it saves on damaged film and possibly lost segments of the film. This type of projector will be of great help to the teacher who is not familiar with projection equipment.

Scuorzo (1967) recommends showing a film in the classroom rather than in a special room for viewing films. Films should be shown where they are part of the educational process, as in the physical education setting. A student must be able to know that he can at least attempt what he sees on the screen in the classroom, gymnasium, on the field or at home.

The use of sound films should be at the descretion of the teacher. He must first preview all films for physical skill levels, educational levels and sound quality. Some groups of students would certainly gain much from a film with sound, whereas some groups of students would gain more from a silent film with the addition of teacher narration.

Slow motion, reverse and stop-action position devices should be part of the motion picture projector. The slow motion position is a very valuable addition when the teacher wishes to emphasize the action of a certain skill in more detail. Students can take the added time to examine the pictures and still have the skill explained to them. The reverse device is good to have in order to rapidly review a skill, action of certain players, or an interesting point in the film. It should also be used when a student presents a question to the teacher about a part of the film which is not clear to him. The stop-action position device is excellent to stop the action of a skill at a precise moment when a crucial point in the skill should be emphasized. For example, the arm position in the delivery of the ball in bowling can be stopped just at the time of release.

These three additions to a movie projector are not frills, but rather necessary items for the best possible piece of audiovisual equipment.

Polaroid Land cameras have their own advantages to add to the adapted physical education program. One very good use for these photographs is on bulletin boards. Student skill progression charts can be preceded by a photograph of the student. In this case, black and white prints are recommended because of the lower cost.

An automatic slide projector which can convert to manual use is best in the physical education setting. This type of projector should also have a forward and reverse direction switch. Some slide containers hold up to three dozen slides which would permit the teacher to show a simple to advanced skill progression. Of course, not all the slides in the container have to be used. Another advantage of this type of slide projector is that the students can operate it by themselves, after receiving instructions from the teacher. Once the names of the switches have been learned, some students will be able to successfully operate the projector at a teaching station.

The preceding suggestions have been ways the teacher can benefit from and use various types of cameras and projectors. Each device is meant to be an addition to the ideal educational setting.

FIELD TRIPS

A field trip is an excellent occasion for utilizing audiovisual aids. Polaroid Land cameras, motion picture cameras and still cameras are to be used on many, if not all, of the field trips a teacher might take throughout the year. The factors which would determine what camera to use are the overall conditions at the scene and whether it is an outside or inside location.

It is a good idea to have a recorded pictorial sequence of the field trip to show the students as a follow-up to the event. Taking a picture of the students as they board the bus would be an excellent point of reference for the students. One or two pictures of familiar sites along the way will bring the students to the next scene, which can be the intended site of the field trip. Once there, a picture of the building, field or activity area would be a good idea. Remember to take pictures at a relatively close distance.

Small objects mean very little to the viewer. Students need to be able to identify the surroundings in the photograph. When using a motion picture camera, remember to move it slowly from one area to another. Stay on the student for a few seconds, at least, before moving to the next scene.

It is very important to consider the field trip site well in advance. Other than the usual concerns of a field trip such as bus accomodations, food, restrooms and the like, the teacher should be aware of the physical nature of the site. If you are taking a class of physically handicapped youngsters on a field trip, you should first consider the terrain. Can the students move their wheelchairs over the site, or do they need assistance? This is one of the main concerns in the field trip.

Students in wheelchairs should be able to view the activity from a good vantage point. Lighting and any natural or man-made barriers should be considered before a class is taken on a field trip. These conditions will also have some bearing on the types of cameras that can be used.

Sporting goods factories make excellent field trip sites. It would be exciting for a class to view the making of baseballs, footballs, golf clubs and bowling balls. A trip to one of these manufacturing centers would enhance the experience of each student in the unit and the unit as well. The teacher can take many unique and interesting photographs on a trip to one of these areas.

There are very few sporting events that occur during the school day. Many take place after school, at night or on weekends. This makes going to a school or professional sporting event almost out of the question. Full advantage must be taken of all recreational and sporting areas in the vicinity of the school and within permissible limits.

Two popular recreational areas used for field trips by public schools, residential settings and day training centers are bowling lanes and miniature golf courses. If the school is in a mild climate, then more outdoor areas can be used for a longer time, but if the setting is in a colder climate, then indoor areas must be sought. However, this is not always the case. Some warm areas have indoor ice skating on a year-round basis, for example.

Another factor the teacher has to take into account is the transportation of adapted physical education equipment. The reader should realize that many of the recreational establishments will not have adapted equipment. The activity will determine the types and amount of special devices needed.

FILMS AND FILMSTRIPS

Films and filmstrips should be used when students can gain a better understanding of the subject matter than they would by using some other audiovisual aid. Both the film and filmstrip can be used in various ways to augment the teaching unit.

Silent, color or black and white motion pictures allow the student to concentrate his attention on the activity presented before him. A motion picture used for the retarded student should not contain any abstract instructions or directions. If this is not the case, for any reason, then the instructor should take on the role as narrator. When a film of this type is used at a teaching station, it should have clear and concise narration, with the activity on the screen being clearly understood by the student. For these reasons alone, the teacher must preview each film and select those that apply to his class. Remember, these teaching stations are designed so students can use the films with as much independence as possible. Before the students view any films, they should be familiar with terms and phrases used in the specific activity. These terms and phrases are those used in the film and by the teacher.

The filmstrip is an excellent teaching device and can be developed into a good teaching station. The filmstrip allows the student to proceed at a pace that is his own. Many filmstrip projectors can be used in a lighted room with the use of a daylight screen. The projectors for filmstrips have become very easy machines to operate. It would be best for the teacher to set the filmstrip in the projector to be ready for use by the student. All the student would have to do is wind the filmstrip frame by frame until it reaches the end. He can rewind it before he moves to the next station.

Students should have the filmstrip explained to them prior to viewing it. They should also be told what things to look for in the filmstrip. As the student develops additional skills in utilizing audiovisual aids, he will enjoy the activity because it has provided him with a successfully independent experience.

LOOP FILMS

A loop film is a single concept film, either sound or silent. Its duration can be from three to five minutes. The film is in a sealed plastic cartridge with both ends of the film spliced together, so that rewinding is not needed. There is no need for extra reels with this cartridge. The length of the film is generally fifty feet, but some are longer. The three excellent advantages of the loop film are no threading, rewinding or complicated loading. A special loop film projector is needed in order to show the film. Another advantage of this type of aid is the compactness of the film cartridge. Many cartridges can be stored in a relatively small cabinet or closet. They do not take up very much room, thus gaining added storage space for other articles.

In the past, this author has used the console type of loop film projector and found it to have many practical features. For one, all the controls are in front, where even the student in a wheelchair can reach them when the console is on a table. The film loads from the back or side, and the screen and projector are in one single unit. It looks very much like a television. There is no problem of where to place the screen or the projector. The console type can also be used in a lighted room, for in many cases it has a daylight screen.

There are other types of loop film projectors and screen combinations available. Some have the screen folded into a case containing both screen and projector. There are individual loop film projectors as well. All are practical for certain areas and under certain circumstances. The reader will have to determine which one suits his needs.

The principal idea of the loop film is to show one phase of a particular skill. The skill could be presented at normal speed and in slow motion on the same loop film. This gives the student a chance to study it step by step and see it as it should be performed.

Loop films can be used in almost any physical education unit or recreational activity. The gymnasium or indoor activity area

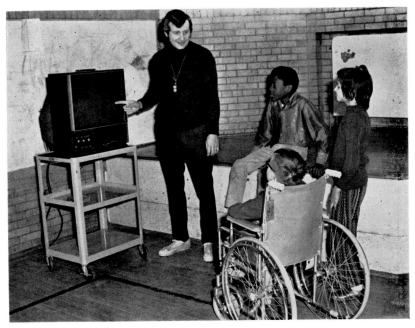

Loop film console.

are the two locations where the films would be used most. It is best to have the loop film equipment set up on a table or movable cart, away from the ongoing activity. In an instance such as this, the loop film projection equipment and film are, in effect, a teaching station. Each teaching station has a different progression or phase of the activity for the students to view and then practice.

The instructor in the photograph above is explaining the use of the console model loop film projector to a small group of students at one of the teaching stations in the gymnasium. All of these students are from a class for the physically handicapped. Notice how the console is transported on a roll-away cart which is an ideal piece of equipment.

At one time or another, many teachers have wished to have a film of a physical education activity that truly applies to their students. It is difficult to purchase a loop film showing a physically handcapped student performing a certain physical education skill. The solution to this problem is for the teacher to make his own loop film. The cost of making a loop film is relatively small one. Advance (1970) mentions that he has made his at a cost of five dollars. This price included the fifty feet of film, processing the film and the cartridging of the film. You can save a considerable sum by filming the activity yourself.

When you plan to make a loop film for a specific group, it is best to use one of your own students. This student should have mastered the use of a certain piece of adapted equipment before the film is made. An example of this would be the student in a wheelchair who has acquired the ability to use a bowling ramp by himself. This student can demonstrate the aiming and the ball retrieving procedures in a film. Keep in mind that there are only three to five minutes in each loop film cartridge. It would be a good idea, also, to have student on crutches demonstrating how to retrieve and deliver a bowling ball; this way, many of the physically handicapped students will see how they might be able to take part in this and other related activities.

The loop film should be taken in a setting familiar to the students. The gymnasium and playground at school are well suited for this purpose. Certain activities will have to be taken at other sites, such as bowling lane, miniature golf course and at a fishing dock. These are activity areas that cannot be duplicated at the school for the most part. The same student can be used for the initial loop film at the school and at the actual recreational site.

Language development can be enhanced through the use of loop films. Simple written commands can accompany a sequence in the film. For example, when the student in the film demonstrates how to swing at a ball on a batting T, a sign can read "LOOK AT THE BALL." Some skills need only one word to describe the action. An example of this is the word "PULL" in archery. These are various ways to use the loop film equipment in the physical education setting. The author is confident that every concerned teacher will be out with his camera taking pictures to use as visual aids for his students.

TAPE RECORDERS

One of the most functional tape recorders to use is the cassette type. This recorder allows the widest range of student use. There is no tape to thread, no reels, and no chance of damaging the tape because it is in a plastic cartridge. The controls on the tape recorder are simple to use. Controls on the recorder are usually the push-button type which would allow the physically handicapped student to use them with a degree of ease. Some of the controls are color-cued for additional ease of operation.

The portable recorder is the most versatile type to use in the physical education setting. It would be best if the recorder was a dual operational cassette; that is it should allow operation by batteries or by plugging into electrical current.

The tape pack, which is the cartridge, is easily stored because of its size and shape. A specially designed tape storage cabinet should be made so a student in a wheelchair could obtain a tape pack from it without leaving his chair. There need not be two separate storage compartments, but instead one cabinet that all students can use.

Teachers can make their own instructional tape recordings for varied activity units. Directions, music and a combination of both can be included on the tape. When the teacher makes his own tape, he is assured of having instructions presented to his students which they can understand and follow. It is best, in this author's opinion, to have the teacher first present new material and instructions to the students, rather than presenting it via audiovisual aids. In any unit of instruction, it is best to review the last day's lesson at the beginning of the present lesson. This is where the tape recorder can be used most effectively by the student.

The cassette tape player will make an excellent teaching station. Directions can be placed on the tape for certain drills or exercises. Music can also be placed on the tape for a movement exploration or dance unit. A student at the station can turn the recorder on and the group then attempts to do what is on the tape. It is an easy task for the students to play back a segment of the tape they need to hear once more. These are certain examples of units where the tape recorder can be used.

The portable tape recorder is excellent for outdoor use when the teacher cannot be in one place for all of the class period. Certain outdoor activities can be enhanced by the use of cassette tape recorders. A few of these are field hockey, croquet, miniature golf and track and field events.

Swimming activities can also benefit from the use of a cassette tape recorder. The teacher can place simple dry land drills on the tape for a small group of students to use. As one group is conducting its lesson in the pool, the other group is receiving a review lesson of the last class meeting from the tape.

There is still another type of tape and filmstrip player. This unit can show filmstrips and provide sound as well. The screen and speaker are contained in one case on some of the models. With this device, the teacher can show a filmstrip without sound and prepare his own narration. When the teacher uses this device with sound, he will probably be using the record that came with the filmstrip. The only thing the teacher will have to be concerned about is to make sure the information on the record applies to his students and also that it is on their level of academic achievement. If the record is not applicable to the students, the teacher will then have to supply the narration.

Cassettes can be used to record student-made projects. A rhythmic music segment can be recorded and played back to the class for its enjoyment. This same musical presentation can be presented at a parent-teacher meeting at which time the parents can hear of some of the activities the class has presented as a project.

The degree of involvement of the tape recorder, either cassette or reel type, will depend on many factors. Some of these factors have been discussed in this section along with their application to a unit of instruction in the adapted physical education program. The teacher should always keep in mind that the tape recorder does not take the place of direct teacher-student involvement, but rather acts as an additional source of information supplied by the teacher. It should be used in a teaching station arrangement, with simple directions furnished for a series of skills.

GUEST SPEAKERS

Guest speakers serve many worthwhile purposes. They add excitement to a unit of instruction by relating their experiences to the students. The guest speaker can demonstrate skills in a specific acivity or he can demonstrate varied pieces of equipment.

A coach from a nearby school athletic team can bring some of his players to school to demonstrate various skills in their sport. The sport they are demonstrating should correspond with the unit of instruction the class is in at that time. The guest speaker could be a handicapped person demonstrating recreational or sport skills to handicapped children. A sporting goods representative could show the students some physical education equipment. Whichever of these guest speakers is presiding over the special program, the emphasis should be on how the students can utilize the information and materials presented to them.

Guest speakers need not come to your school, necessarily, but rather you can go to their facility. Sometimes, the guest speaker is unable to come to your setting and you must go to his. This venture can be considered both a guest speaker appearance and a field trip.

An example of a guest speaker activity would be a wheelchair basketball team performing for and instructing handicapped students. The program can be separated into three segments consisting of a demonstration, a performance of a short game, and instructing the students on a few skills in basketball. In this instruction, the student might try some of the skills the guests have demonstrated. At this point in the program, it would be vital for the students to have an opportunity to use some of the guest's adapted equipment. It would certainly mean a great deal if the guests worked right along with the students.

If time and circumstances permit, the guests can participate in a fun-type game of basketball as a culmination of this special program. The reader is reminded to take motion pictures and still photographs of some of the program to use as instructional material and a source of discussion with the students.

Mentally retarded students would also enjoy a similar sports presentation by a group of high school bowling players, for example. It certainly would be ideal if the program could be held at a local bowling establishment during the day. Many bowling establishments may not be so busy during the school day, and could perhaps accomodate such a program. The bowling team's coach and the physical education teacher could coordinate the specific skills which each will work on during the course of the program. The high school team can demonstrate the basic skills either in the bowling lanes or in the gymnasium. After the initial demonstration, the high school students should work with a few of the students in various aspects of the game. As a final activity, the high school students each choose a partner from the class and bowl a game together.

Guest speakers can also bring in films to show to the students on many different recreational sports activities. These activities can be of camping sites and facilities there, or public recreational sites and their facilities. All of these areas should be of concern to the student as they apply to his handicap.

These are just a few of the ways guest speakers can be used and how they can influence the success of the unit. The degree of outside involvement of other personnel will depend upon the teacher and his desire to make the unit of instruction a most meaningful one for his students. This author believes that the above methods of using guest speakers are very successful ways in which to encourage the handicapped child's participation in recreational activities.

RECORD PLAYERS

The record player is probably one of the most used aids in the physical education program. There are records of musical games, instructions, dances and exercises, to list a few. It is no wonder then that record players are an important consideration in the adapted physical education program.

The manual and automatic record players are the two main types used in the physical education program. The controls of the manual record player should consist of on, volume, speed selector and pause control.

The pause control is used when the teacher wishes to stop the record to give additional instructions, but does not want to lift the tone arm off of the record and lose his place. When the pause control is disengaged, the record resumes playing.

The automatic record player has the above mentioned controls with the exception of the pause control selector.

Because many records used in the physical education class

come in the 45 rpm speed, it is best to have a built-in 45 rpm adapter. This adapter is built into the base of the spindle and can be raised for 45 rpm records and lowered for other records. In this way, the chance of losing an adapter is eliminated.

The teacher in charge of ordering equipment for the physical education department should consider who will be using the record player. If it is the teacher only, then the manual type would be best in this author's opinion. However, if his students will be using a record player, different considerations will have to be made. Manual dexterity and knowledge of how to use a record player are key considerations to student operation of valuable equipment . In a situation like this, the best type of record player to use with physically handicapped students is the manual type. The chance of equipment damage is lessened because of the simple operation of the device. Many times the control mechanism is a knob with an indicator directing the student which way to turn it for a desired effect. Certainly, before the students operate the record player, they would have been instructed in its use. A competent student in each group or at each teaching station can be in charge of the operation of the record player.

For safety and storage feasibility, the record player should be on a portable rolling table that has at least two shelves. The lower shelf would be for those students who can operate the record player from a wheelchair and the upper shelf would be for those students who can function from a standing position. The record player should be kept on the roller table for use in the class and for storage as well. This will eliminate excessive handling and the chance of damaging the equipment.

The students using the record player should be at one end of the gymnasium, while the remaining students are at the other end. The group using the record player can be in a corner of the gymnasium with the volume turned down so it will not distract the other students.

Records should be introduced to the entire class before the members separate into groups. Many times, records are intended for the use of the entire class. The records used at a teaching station could be directions for the execution of simple skills.

The preceding are ways in which the teacher can use the

record player in the adapted physical education program. Here, the emphasis is placed on maximizing the individual's skill development in many areas.

CULMINATING ACTIVITIES

$\mathbf{T}$HE CULMINATION OF A teaching unit must be an activity that exemplifies the entire unit. This is where all that has been learn-ed by the student is exhibited to spectators or used in other ways. During a culminating activity, pupils are brought together to demonstrate their new skills to friends, teachers and their families (Daughtrey, 1967).

These culminating activities can take the form of a demonstra-tion, show, competition or field trip. Each is just as important and valuable to a teaching unit. Any one of the culminating activities can be more involved than the others, but each is an exciting end-ing to an enjoyable unit.

DEMONSTRATIONS

For use in this book, a demonstration is an activity where students present new physical skills they have learned to a group of spectators. The use of adapted equipment will depend on the activity being presented, and on who is giving the demonstration. In a demonstration, the new skills are presented in a ladder form. Students demonstrate the basic steps to a skill, and then proceed to the execution of a more advanced skill. The use of equipment in this culminating activity is also dealt with in the same way.

Usually, demonstrations will be held close to or on the same site where the skills were acquired. Such places would be the gymnasium, outdoor field or special activity room.

A commentator is present at a demonstration and his role is to describe the activity to the audience. He will also describe the basic skills that have been learned and the ensuing advanced skills leading to the final or desired skill. The commentator in most cases should be the person who is in charge of the program, or the person who performed the actual teaching. It would be best if the person in charge had an assistant to help with the equipment and students as he describes what is taking place before the audience. Demonstrations also give a firsthand account of the purposes and objectives of the program (Daughtrey, 1967) as well as the use of adapted physical education equipment.

Students should demonstrate how they use any adapted equipment. At this time, the students could show each phase of the operation of a device. A demonstration is a very factual presentation of skills and the use of adapted physical education equipment. The student takes the audience from his basic or initial phase to his present level of physical achievement.

COMPETITIONS

Competitions should always be designed so that each member taking part in a contest will enjoy himself. The main idea of having a competitive event is to determine a winner. This author prefers first, second, third and fourth place winners, instead of saying someone lost. The use of the phrase "last place" is to be discouraged. No one enjoys being in last place, especially in the culmination of a unit.

There are various types of competitions. Some of these include one class versus another, one person versus another, one team versus another, one team versus another within a single class, and a school team versus another school team. All but the last form can be conducted in one school building. Competitions in a residential setting will be discussed later in this section.

Whatever the competition happens to be, the teacher must be sure that opponents are matched according to capabilities, age and sex insofar as possible. The type of adapted device being used will have a great influence on which two persons are matched together. Bowling would be a fine example of this. Here one student could use a push device and the other student could use a board or ramp. Both would be using an adapted device to bring them to a level of competency.

An intramural program can be in one school building or in a residential setting. Individual and team activities can be conducted on a large scale. Trophies, plaques and ribbons could be issued to the individual winners or teams. There should be at least five winning places in each event of a contest. In this way, more students would have an opportunity to win a ribbon, or whatever the award may be. It is a good idea to present the student with a certificate along with his other award, as this gives the student something he can exhibit on his wall at home or in his classroom.

It would add a lot to the contest if the team members wore some sort of team uniform. These uniforms can be made by the students, who also select the colors and the name of the team. Imagine all the skills involved in preparing the uniforms: arithmetical concepts, language development, shape discrimination, hand-eye coordination and the use of small hand tools. The actual making of a uniform and wearing it in competition is an exciting experience for the student who has not been involved in such a venture.

The competitive spirit exists in the retarded and physically handicapped as it does in the normal child. Truly, the emphasis is not on winning, but on being able to participate in a normal part of life. It is this author's belief that the exceptional child should not be excluded from competition simply because he might lose, or worse yet, because he might be injured. If all safety precautions have been taken, or planned for, the teacher can proceed with a full program for the handicapped child.

In the past, this author has conducted floor hockey tournaments for physically handicapped boys and girls. Boys did not compete with or against girls. These tournaments were the culmination of the hockey unit. Each student, no matter how severe his condition, had a place on his team. Other classrooms and parents were invited to the games, and this made for a pleasant affair.

At a residential setting, the number of students in the physical education program is larger than in most special education schools. There could be two or three teams from each dormitory or cottage in the residential facility. One cottage can compete with another and one dormitory can compete with another. The reader should consider the tremendous amount of student involvement that can be produced by having an intramural program within each cottage.

The students can be completely involved in the program by being able to select any activity they wish to participate in from the variety of individual and team sports. By presenting a vast number of activities, many students, if not all, are participating.

Competition gives the individual an opportunity to succeed by himself or as a member of a team. Many times, the adapted physical education device, which is suited to the handicapped student, will allow him to enter a new world of physical interests—especially in a competitive event.

SHOWS

Shows are exclusively for entertainment. The show is primarily designed to bring attention to the variety of skills each student has acquired. The students' costumes should be elaborate and colorful. The show should also include brightly decorated program books, music of different types for the variety of acts, and room decorations. Each student has an opportunity to be in many segments of a show, regardless of his handicap. Some of the acts in which he can appear are a square dance act with wheelchairs, a gymnastics act, a folk dance act, a girls' precision dance act and a finale. These are some of the acts used by this author for presentation to parents, friends, teachers and relatives of the students in the show.

Two, and possibly three, shows a year are adequate. This is recommended for three reasons. First, if the teacher waited until the end of the year for the one and only show, he would have to reteach many of the skills in each unit, beginning with the first. Certainly, some of the students will retain many skills, but the goal is for all to take part. Second, if more than three shows took place in a year, the effect of the show would be minimized and not much instruction of skills would take place. Most of the time would be spent preparing for the show. Last, two shows is the optimum number for one year. After a four-month period, a majority of students will have developed many physical skills, as well as ability to use various pieces of adapted equipment. Instead of squeezing all of the year's units into one show and not really doing any of the units justice, two shows can demonstrate the year's work most effectively.

Shows can take place in the gymnasium or on a stage. In some schools, the stage is in the gymnasium. Where the show is performed would largely depend upon the type of activities in the show and the equipment and facilities needed.

Other areas where shows can be presented are children's and Veterans Administration hospitals, senior citizens residences, and in other schools and hospitals. These are the places this author has utilized, gaining the most positive response for both entertainers and spectators.

The mention of a show excites not only the student, but his family and friends as well. This is a fine opportunity to seek the aid of parents. It gives them a chance to work with their children in a mutually rewarding experience. It is one thing for a parent to see his child become an active member of a class because of the equipment, but it is another for the parent to work right along with the child and see how he has learned to use the special equipment.

Pieces of equipment can be painted and decorated to appear exceptionally vivid and outstanding. Wheelchairs, crutches and canes can be individually decorated by the student in school or at home. Parents should only assist the child with his creation and not make it a parent creation. Costumes can also be made in school or at home with parent help. The gymnasium can be decorated by the students with some of their own paintings and posters. This makes the show theirs, not the teacher's. Whatever the theme of the show happens to be, it is the entertainment provided by the student for his family and friends that is most important. A program like this gives the student an opportunity to show off for those close to him.

FIELD TRIPS

Field trips can also be used as culminating activities. There will be those instances where an outstanding and meaningful culmination to a unit of instruction can take place outside of the school setting.

A field trip can consist of eating lunch in a restaurant, touring a sports equipment factory related to the unit the class is in, and participating in actual physical activity. For example, a trip to a golf equipment manufacturing plant can be made in the morning, followed by lunch. Then the students can play a round of miniature golf at a nearby miniature golf course. Any adapted equipment can be brought along to use. After the game of golf, the students go back to school. This is a total educational experience.

The reader has been informed of various ways that culminating activities can be utilized to bring a unit of instruction to an enjoyable close. The uses of specialized pieces of equipment have been discussed in terms of how they fit into the total scheme of shows, demonstrations, competitions and field trips. In all of the above culminating activities, the teacher should remember to take various kinds of photographs. These include still photographs and motion pictures. It is up to the teacher to broaden the program of adapted physical education for mentally and physically handicapped children, teenagers and adults. Parents, fellow teachers, administrators and, of course, the students themselves should be able to look back on each unit and remember the excitement of the culminating activity. It should leave a lasting effect on the minds and bodies of the students involved in the adapted physical education program.

BIBLIOGRAPHY

1. Adams, D. Raymond, Denny-Brown, D. and Pearson, Carl M.: *Disease of Muscle*. New York, Paul B. Hoeber, Inc., 1954.
2. Athletic Institute and American Association for Health, Physical Education and Recreation: *Equipment and Supplies for Athletics, Physical Education and Recreation*. Chicago and Washington, D.C. 1960.
3. Avance, Lyonel D.: Film loops enhance handicapped physical education program. *ICRH Newsletter, 4*:1:1970.
4. Baker, Harvey J.: *Introduction to Exceptional Children*. 2nd ed. New York, Macmillan Co., 1953.
5. Blake, Florence G. and Wright, F. Howell: *Essentials of Pediatric Nursing*. Philadelphia, J. B. Lippincott Co., 1963.
6. Brown, James W., Lewis, Richard B. and Harceroad, Fred F.: *Audio-Visual Instruction—Media and Methods*, 3rd ed. New York, McGraw-Hill Book Co., 1969.
7. Bryce, Margaret: *Physical Therapy After Amputation—The Treatment of the Unilateral Lower-Extremity Amputee*. Madison, The University of Wisconsin Press, 1954.
8. Bucher, Charles A.: *Foundations of Physical Education*, 5th ed. St. Louis, The C. V. Mosby Co., 1968.
9. Buell, Charles E.: *Physical Education for Blind Children*. Springfield, Charles C. Thomas, 1966.
10. Cruickshank, William M. and Johnson, G. Orville: *Education of Exceptional Children and Youth*, 2nd ed. Englewood Cliffs, Prentice-Hall, Inc., 1967.
11. Daniels, Arthur S.: *Adapted Physical Education—Principals and Practice of Physical Education for Exceptional Students*. New York, Harper and Brothers, 1954.
12. Daughtrey, Greyson: *Methods in Physical Education and Health for Secondary Schools*. Philadelphia, W. B. Saunders Co., 1967.
13. Erickson, Carlton W. H.: *Fundamentals of Teaching with Audio-Visual Technology*. New York, Macmillan Co., 1965.
14. Fait, Hollis, F.: *Adapted Physical Education*. Philadelphia, W. B. Saunders Co., 1960.
15. Fait, Hollis F.: *Special Physical Education—Adaptive, Corrective*

and *Developmental*, 2nd ed. Philadelphia, W. B. Saunders Co., 1966.

16. Godfrey, Barbara B. and Kephart, Newell C.: *Movement Patterns and Motor Education.* New York, Appleton-Century-Crofts, 1969, p. 198.

17. Goldenshon, Eli S. and Barrows, Howard S.: *Handbook for Patients.* New York, Ayerest Laboratories.

18. Graton, Malinda Dean: *Teaching the Educable Mentally Retarded*, 2nd ed. Springfield, Charles C. Thomas, 1964.

19. Grulee, Clifford G. and Eley, R. Cannon: *The Child In Health and Disease.* Baltimore, The Williams and Wilkins Co., 1952.

20. Horkheimer, A. P.: *Educators Guide to Free Films*, 2nd ed. Randolph, Wisconsin, Educators Progress Service, 1969.

21. Irwin, Leslie W.: *The Curriculum in Health and Physical Education*, 2nd ed. St. Louis, The C. V. Mosby Co., 1951.

22. Jones, Edwina, Morgan, Edna and Stevens, Gladys: *Methods and Materials in Elementary Physical Education.* Yonkers-on-Hudson, World Book Co., 1957.

23. Keats, Sidney: *Cerebral Palsy.* Springfield, Charles C. Thomas, 1965.

24. Kirchner, Glenn: *Physical Education for Elementary School Children.* Dubuque, William C. Brown Co., 1966.

25. Kirk, Samuel A.: *Education of Exceptional Children.* Boston, Houghton Mifflin Co., 1962.

26. Kirk, Samuel A. and Johnson, G. Orville: *Educating the Retarded Child.* Cambridge, Houghton Mifflin Co., 1951.

27. Livingston, Samuel: *Living With Epileptic Seizures.* Springfield, Charles C. Thomas, 1963.

28. Mathews, Donald K., Kruse, Robert and Shaw, Virginia: *The Science of Physical Education for Handicapped Children.* New York, Harper and Brothers, 1962.

29. Merrill, Toni: *Activities for the Aged and Infirm—A Handbook for the Untrained Worker.* Springfield, Charles C. Thomas, 1967.

30. Nelson, E. Waldo, Vaughan, Victor C. III and McKay, R. James: *Textbook of Pediatrics*, 9th ed., Philadelphia, W. B. Saunders Co., 1969.

31. Newman, Judy: Swimming for the spina bifida. *Programs for Handicapped*, 6;1970..

32. Peters, Laurence J.: *Prescriptive Teaching.* New York, McGraw-Hill Book Co., 1965.

33. Rathbone, Josephine L. and Lucas, Carol: *Recreation in Total Rehabilitation.* Springfield, Charles C. Thomas, 1959.

34. Robinson, Halbert B. and Robinson, Nancy M.: *The Mentally Retarded Child.* New York, McGraw-Hill Book Co., 1965.
35. Rothwell, Angus B.: *A Guide to Curriculum Building in Physical Education.* Curriculum Bulletin Number 28. Madison, State of Wisconsin, 1963.
36. Scuorzo, Herbert E.: *The Practical Audio-Visual Handbook for Teachers.* West Nyack Parker Publishing Co., 1967.
37. Shafer, Kathleen Newton, Sawyer, Janet R., McClusky, Audrey M. and Beck, Edna Lifgren: *Medical-Surgical Nursing.* St. Louis, The C. V. Mosby Co., 1962.
38. State of Michigan: *Making Facilities Accessible for the Physically Handicapped,* Act Number 1 of the Public Acts of 1966. Lansing, Michigan, 1966.
39. Stone, L. and Church, Joseph: *Childhood and Adolescence,* New York, Random House, 1957.

Manufacturers of Indoor and Outdoor Physical Education Equipment and Supplies

THE FOLLOWING IS a list of equipment and supplies for units of instruction in adapted and regular physical education. Each firm in this general listing has supplies for many, if not all of the traditional physical education activites.

A B C School Supply
34 E. Andrews Dr.
Atlanta, Georgia 30305

American Athletic Equipment
Pinet and McKinley Streets
Jefferson, Iowa 50129

American Import Co.
1167 Mission St.
San Francisco, California 94103

American Youth Marketing Corp.
Alms Building
Cincinnati, Ohio 45206

Archer Plastics, Inc.
1125 Close Ave.
Bronx, New York 10451

Arrow Rubber and Plastics
Box 104
West Englewood, New Jersey 07666

Athletic Trainers Supply Co.
427 Broadway
New York, New York 10027

Bailey Manufacturing Co.
P. O. Box 38
Lodi, Ohio 44254

Banner Plastics Corp.
80 Beckwith Ave.
Paterson, New Jersey 07503

Barr Rubber Products Co.
Sandusky, Ohio 44870

Battle Creek Equipment Co.
307 W. Jackson St.
Battle Creek, Michigan 49016

Belson Manufacturing
North Aurora, Illinois 60542

Birdair Structures
1800-10 Broadway
Buffalo, New York 14212

Bolco Athletic Co.
1751 N. Eastern Ave.
Log Angeles, California 90032

BUC-OL Manufacturing
1017 S. Locust St.
Oxford, Ohio 45056

Childcraft Equipment Co., Inc.
155 E. 23rd St.
New York, New York 10027

Childhood Interest, Inc.
Roselle Park, New Jersey 07203

Childplay of New York, Inc.
203 W. 14th St.
New York, New York 10027

Children's Music Center, Inc.
5373 W. Pico Blvd.
Los Angeles, California 90003

Community Playthings
Rifton, New York 12471

Cooperative Recreation Service, Inc.
Radnor Rd.
Delaware, Ohio 43015

Crosman Arms Co.
E. Church St.
Fairport, New York 14450

Daval Rubber Co.
Providence, Rhode Island 02900

Dayton Racquet Co.
936 Albright St.
Arcanum, Ohio 45304

Developmental Learning Materials
3505 N. Ashland Ave.
Chicago, Illinois 60657

Andy Douglas, Inc.
2758 Orchid St.
New Orleans, Louisiana 70119

Dudley Sports Co., Inc.
12-12 37th Ave.
Long Island City, New York 11102

Form, Inc.
12900 W. 10 Mile Rd.
South Lyon, Michigan 48178

Fun and Fitness, Inc.
Box FF
Montezuma, Iowa 50171

General Playground Equipment, Inc.
1139 S. Courtland Ave.
Kokomo, Indiana 46901

Giant Manufacturing Co.
Council Bluffs, Iowa 51501

Gong Bell Co.
East Hampton, Connecticut
200 Fifth Ave.
New York, New York 10027

Groler Industries, Inc.
35-47 31st St.
Long Island City, New York 11102

Gym Master Co.
3200 S. Luni St.
Englewood, Colorado 80110

Harrington & Richardson, Inc.
320 Park Ave.
Worchester, Massachusetts 01610

Delmar F. Harris Co.
P. O. Box 288
Concordia, Kansas 66901

Hillerich & Bradsby Co.
P. O. Box 506
Louisville, Kentucky 40201

Earl H. Hurley Associates
162 Maple Ave.
Corry, Pennsylvania 16407

Ideal Toy Corp.
200 Fifth Ave.
New York, New York 10027

International Fiberglass Co.
1038 Princeton Dr.
Venice, California 90291

Irwin Corp.
85 Factory St.
Nashua, New Hampshire 03060

Alan Jay
3547 Webster Ave.
New York, New York 10027

Herbert Jennings
Box 308
Litchfield, Michigan 49252

Jolly Toys, Inc.
459 West 15 St.
New York, New York 10027

Kiefer-McNeil
2741 Wingate Ave.
Akron, Ohio 44314

Killebrew, Inc.
68 S. Main
Salt Lake City, Utah 84101

Knickerbocker Toy Co.
1107 Broadway
New York, New York 10027

Lomma Enterprises, Inc.
305 Cherry St.
Scranton, Pennsylvania 18501

Lumex, Inc.
Bellmore, New York 11710

3-M Company
367 Grove St.
St. Paul, Minnesota 55101

MacGregor/Brunswick
Interstate 75 at Jimson Rd.
Cincinnati, Ohio 45215

Mansfield-Zesiger Manufacturing Co.
Cuyahoga Falls, Ohio 44221

Marcy Gymnasium Equipment Co.
1736 Standard Ave.
Glendale, California 91201

Masenfield Bros., Inc.
Center Falls, Rhode Island 02863

Mason City Tent and Awning Co.
406 S. Federal
Mason City, Iowa 50401

Master Lock Co.
2600 N. 32nd St.
Milwaukee, Wisconsin 53245

Melrose Manufacturing Co.
95 Commercial St.
Brookline, New York 11212

Mitchell Division
Royal Industries
1500 E. Chestnut St.
Santa Ana, California 92701

National Sports Co.
362 N. Marquette St.
Fond du Lac, Wisconsin 54935

Nevco Score Board Co.
Greenville, Illinois 62246

Niedermeyer-Martin Co.
1727 N. E. 11th Ave.
Portland, Oregon 97212

Passon's, Inc.
824 Arch St.
Philadelphia, Pennsylvania 19107

Physical Education Equipment Aids
P. O. Box 5117
San Mateo, California 94402

Playcrete Co.
185 N. 15th St.
Bloomfield, New Jersey 07003

Playground Corporation of America
29-16 40th Ave.
Long Island City, New York 11101

Playtime Products
Warsaw, Indiana 46580

Play Street, Inc.
555 Madison Ave.
New York, New York 10027

Play Systems, Inc.
919 N. Michigan Ave.
Chicago, Illinois 60611

Plymouth Golf Ball Co.
Butler Pike
Plymouth Meeting, Pennsylvania 19462

Pomona Service and Supply Co.
2310 Fruitvale Blvd.
Yakima, Washington 98902

J. A. Preston Corp.
71 Fifth Ave.
New York, New York 10003

Program Aids, Inc.
No. 1 Physical Fitness Drive
Garden City, New York 11530

Recreational Equipment Co.
724 W. 8th St.
Anderson, Indiana 46011

Resilite Sports Products, Inc.
P. O. Box 442
Sunbury, Pennsylvania 17801

Rocky Mountain Metals Corp.
Denver, Colorado 80200

Saunders Archery Co.
P. O. Box 476
Columbus, Nebraska 68601

School Playthings, Inc.
109 W. Hubbard St.
Chicago, Illinois 60602

Sindelar Water Basketball Co.
3619 Hollywood Ave.
Brookfield, Illinois 60513

Smally & Bates, Inc.
425 Park Avenue S.
New York, New York 10027

R. L. Spillman Co.
Box 4167
Columbus, Ohio 43207

Sterling Recreation Products
164 Belmony Ave.
Belleville, New Jersey 07109

Sturdisteel Co.
P. O. Drawer 949
Waco, Texas 76703

Sun Rubber Co.
Barberton, Ohio 44203

Universal Athletic Sales Co.
4707 E. Hedges
Fresno, California 93703

Universe Co.
Altadena, California 91001

Walco Toy Co., Inc.
38 W. 37th St.
New York, New York 10027

Wenger Corp.
37 Wenger Building
Owatonna, Minnesota 55060

Wham-O Manufacturing Co.
835 E. El Monte St.
San Gabriel, California 91778

Equipment and Supplies for Specific Physical Education Activities

Archery

American Archery Co.
Claredon Hills, Illinois 60514

American Excelsior Corp.
850 Avenue H East
Arlington, Texas 76010

Am-Pro, Inc.
5120 Old Clairton Rd.
Pittsburg, Pennsylvania 15200

Anderson Archery Corp.
Grand Ledge, Michigan 48837

Bear Archery Co.
Grayling, Michigan 49738

Browning Arms Co.
Department 576
P. O. Box 500
Morgan, Utah 84050

Walter H. Craig
Box 927
Selma, Alabama 36701

Fish Net and Twine Co.
927 First St.
Menominee, Michigan 49858

Damon Howatt
Archery Manufacturing, Inc.
Route 8
Yakima, Washington 98902

Jayfro Corp.
4 Bridge St.
Montville, Conencticut 06353

Kittridge Bow Hut
P. O. Box 98 T
Mamoth Lakes, California 93546

Ben Pearson
421 N. Atlantic Dr.
Pasadena, California 91107

Realistic Ranges of America
P. O. Box 5237
Fayetteville, North Carolina 28301

Root Archery
Kalamazoo, Michigan 49001

Shakespeare Co.
240 Kalamazoo Ave.
Kalamazoo, Michigan 49001

Superior Net Co.
P. O. Box 237
Highland, Illinois 62249

York Archery
P. O. Box 367
Independence, Missouri 64000

Badminton

Crown Continental Corp.
150 Lafayette St.
New York, New York 10027

Dayton Racquet Co.
710 Albright St.
Arcanum, Ohio 45304

J. E. Gregory Co.
922 W. First
Spokane, Washington 99204

Jamison, Inc.
19253 S. Vermont Ave.
Torrance, California 90509

Jayfro Corp.
4 Bridge St.
Montville, Connecticut 06353

Porter-Leavitt Co.
9555 Irving Park Rd.
Schiller Park, Illinois 60176

Safeway Steel Products
6228 W. State St.
Milwaukee, Wisconsin 53200

Seamless Rubber Co.
253 Hallock Ave.
New Haven, Connecticut 06500

Superior Net Co.
P. O. Box 237
Highland, Illinois 62249

Trojan Playground Equipment
  Manufacturing Co.
11 2nd Avenue, N. E.
St. Cloud, Minnesota 56301

Victory Sports Products
927 First St.
Menominee, Michigan 49858

West Coast Netting, Inc.
14929 Clark Ave.
City of Industry, California 91744

Baseball and Softball

Adirondack Bats, Inc.
McKinley Ave.
Dolgeville, New York 13329

American Playground Device Co.
Nahma, Michigan 49864

R. E. Austin & Son
705 Bedford Ave.
Bellmore, New York 11710

Baseball Grand Slam, Inc.
655 Madison Ave.
New York, New York 10036

Bolco Athletic Co.
1751 N. Eastern Ave.
Los Angeles, California 90003

Cosom Corp.
6030 Wayzata Blvd.
Minneapolis, Minnesota 55400

J. deNeer & Son, Inc.
66 Orange St.
Albany, New York 12201

Dudley Sports Co., Inc.
19 W. 34th St.
New York, New York 10036

General Playground Equipment, Inc.
P. O. Box 608
Kokomo, Indiana 46901

Hanna Manufacturing Co.
Athens, Georgia 30601

H. Harwood & Sons, Inc.
12 Walnut St.
Natick, Massachusetts 01760

Hillerich & Bradsby
434 Finzer Ave.
Louisville, Kentucky 40200

Jamison, Inc.
19253 S. Vermont Ave.
Torrance, California 90500

Lannon Manufacturing Co.
Tullahoma, Tennessee 37388

Marleau-Hercules Fence Co.
3600 Detroit Ave.
Toledo, Ohio 43612

Rawlings Sports Goods Co.
2300 Delmar Blvd.
St. Louis, Missouri 63100

A. G. Spalding & Bros., Inc.
Chicopee, Massachusetts 01020

Stewart Industries
P. O. Box 1039
Cincinnati, Ohio 45200

Trojan Playground Equipment Co.
11 2nd Ave.
St. Cloud, Minnesota 56301

Victory Sports Products
927 First St.
Menominee, Michigan 49858

W. J. Voit Rubber Co.
3801 S. Harbor Blvd.
Santa Ana, California 92700

West Coast Netting, Inc.
14929 Clark Ave.
City of Industry, California 91744

Wilson Sportings Goods, Inc.
2233 West St.
River Grove, Illinois 60171

Basketball

American Playground Device Co.
Nahma, Michigan 49864

Arrow Products Co.
31301 Stephenson Highway
Madison Heights, Michigan 48071

J. E. Burke Co.
P. O. Box 549
Fond du Lac, Wisconsin 54935

Everwear Park and Playground
  Equipment, Inc.
P. O. Box 291
Oconomowoc, Wisconsin 53066

Game-time, Inc.
Litchfield, Michigan 49252

Goshen Manfacturing Co.
P. O. Box 607
Goshen, Indiana 46526

J. E. Gregory Co.
922 W. 1st St.
Spokane, Washington 99200

Jayfro Corp.
4 Bridge St.
Montville, Connecticut 06353

Miracle Equipment Co.
P. O. Box 275
Grinnell, Iowa 50112

Nissen Corp.
930 27th Ave. S. W.
Cedar Rapids, Iowa 52420

Victory Sports Products
927 First St.
Menominee, Michigan 49858

Wilson Sportings Goods, Inc.
2233 West St.
River Grove, Illinois 60171

Billiards

Brunswick Corp.
623 S. Wabash Ave.
Chicago, Illinois 60600

Lomma Enterprises. Inc.
305 Cherry St.
Scranton, Pennsylvania 18500

North American Recreation
  Convertibles, Inc.
P. O. Box 147
Westport, Connecticut 06880

Bowling

Brunswick Corp.
623 S. Wabash Ave.
Chicago, Illinois 60600

Cosom Corp.
6030 Wayzata Blvd.
Minneapolis, Minnesota 55400

Riedel Shoes, Inc.
P. O. Box 21
Red Wing, Minnesota 55060

H. M. Wise Sales Agency
2121 Helen Ave.
Mansville, Ohio 44900

Bulletin Boards

Acme Bulletin and Directory
  Board Corp.
37 E. 12th St.
New York, New York 10027

Beacon Products Co.
4106 N. 24th Place
Milwaukee, Wisconsin 53200

Bestile Manufacturing Co.
621 S. Bonview Ave.
Ontario, California 91761

Brewster, Inc.
Old Lyme, Connecticut 06371

Dayton Stencil Work Co.
113 E. 2nd St.
Dayton, Ohio 45400

Lake Shore Markets, Inc.
P. O. Box 59
Erie, Pennsylvania 16500

Nasco Instructional Materials
901 Jonesville Ave.
Fort Atkinson, Wisconsin 53538

Sargent-Sowell, Inc.
Department PR Box 21
Arlington, Texas 76010

Croquet

Skawhegan Croquet
Wilton, Maine 04294

Dance

Rhythms Production Records
Whitney Building
Los Angeles, California 90003

Fencing

Costello Combative Sports Co.
30 E. 10th St.
New York, New York 10027

Safe Fencing Co.
21 Harrison Ave.
Glen Falls, New York 12801

Fishing

Cosom Corp.
6030 Wayzata Blvd.
Minneapolis, Minnesota 55400

Daisy/Heddon
Rogers, Arkansas 72756

Feather Craft, Inc.
450 Bishop St.
N. W., Atlanta, Georgia 30305

The Garcia Corp.
329 Alfred Ave.
Teaneck, New Jersey 07666

Lake Products Co., Inc.
1254 Grover Rd.
St. Louis, Missouri 63100

Victory Sports Products
927 First St.
Menominee, Michigan 49858

Football

Cosom Corp.
6030 Wayzata Blvd.
Minneapolis, Minnesota 55440

Dudley Sports Co., Inc.
19 W. 34th St.
New York, New York 10036

General Tire and Rubber Co.
Pennsylvania Athletic Products
P. O. Box 591
Akron, Ohio 44300

R. E. Muncey, Inc.
P. O. Box 387
Birmingham, Michigan 48008

Rawlings Sporting Goods Co.
2300 Delmar Blvd.
St. Louis, Missouri 63100

W. J. Voit Rubber Co.
3801 S. Harbor Blvd.
Santa Ana, California 92700

Wilson Sporting Goods Co.
2233 West St.
River Grove, Illinois 60171

Games

All Metal Table Tennis Co.
Box 142, Department A
Teaneck, New Jersey 07666

August Amusement Games, Inc.
7709 Greenview Terrace
Towson, Maryland 21204

Brinktun, Inc.
5740 Wayzata Blvd.
Minneapolis, Minnesota 55400

Carrom Games
1000 Rowe St.
Ludington, Michigan 49431

Cosom Corp.
6030 Wayzata Blvd.
Minneapolis, Minnesota 55400

Creative Ideas Co.
5328 W. 142nd Place
Hawthorne, California 90250

Creative Playthings, Inc.
5757 W. Century Blvd.
Los Angeles, California 90003

Economy Handicrafts, Inc.
Box 210
Little Neck, New York 11363

Educational Activities
1937 Grand Ave.
Baldwin, New York 11510

Electro-Mechanical Industries, Inc.
Box 3721
Washington, D. C. 20005

Gates Manufacturing Co.
P. O. Box 111
Ozark, Arkansas 72949

Lormac Co.
P. O. Box 578
1120 W. Industrial St.
Escondido, California 92025

Mason City Tent and Awning Co.
406 S. Federal Ave.
Mason City, Iowa 50401

North American Recreation
Convertibles, Inc.
P. O. Box 417
Westport, Connecticut 06880

Les Pete Sporting Goods
Box 17181
Portland, Oregon 97200

Sindelar Water Basketball Co.
3619 Hollywood Ave.
Brookfield, Illinois 60513

Skip-Bo, Inc.
Box 5033
Lubbock, Texas 79400

Space-Ball
208 Appleton St.
Holyoke, Massachusetts 01040

Valley Manufacturing and Sales Co.
333 Morton St.
Bay City, Michigan 48706

Wiff 'N Poof Publishers
Box 71
New Haven, Connecticut 06500

World Wide Games
Box 450
Delaware, Ohio 43015

Gymnastics

American Athletic Equipment Co.
Jefferson, Iowa 50129

Atlas Athletic Equipment Co.
2339 Hampton Ave.
St. Louis, Missouri 63139

J. E. Burke Co.
Fond du Lac, Wisconsin 54935

Everwear Park and Playground
  Equipment, Inc.
36535 W. Highway 16
P. O. Box 291
Oconomowoc, Wisconsin 53066

Frank Endo
12200 S. Berendo
Los Angeles, California 90044

Game-time, Inc.
Litchfield, Michigan 49252

Gym Master
3200 S. Luni St.
Englewood, Colorado 80110

Gymnastic Supply Co.
247 W. 6th St.
San Pedro, California 90731

National Sports Co.
351 N. Marquette St.
Fon du Lac, Wisconsin 54936

Nissen Corp.
930 27th Ave. S. W.
Cedar Rapids, Iowa 52420

Porter Corp.
9555 Irving Park Rd.
Schiller Park, Illinois 60175

Premier Products
River Vale, New Jersey 07675

Program Aids Co., Inc.
No. 1 Physical Fitness Dr.
Garden City, New York 11530

Hockey

Charles R. Beltz & Co.
15001 Charlevoix Ave.
Grosse Point Park, Michigan 48236

Cosom Corp.
6030 Wayzata Blvd.
Minneapolis, Minnesota 55400

General Hardware Co.
3618 W. Pierce St.
Milwaukee, Wisconsin 53200

Jayfro Corp.
P. O. Box 50
Montville, Connecticut 06353

R. E. Muncey, Inc.
P. O. Box 387
Birmingham, Michigan 48008

Rinkmasters
P. O. Box 115
Eastchester, New York 10709

Safeway Steel Products
6228 W. State St.
Milwaukee, Wisconsin 53200

Superior Net Co.
P. O. Box 237
Highland, Illinois 62249

Victory Sports Products
927 First St.
Menominee, Michigan 49858

Horseshoes

Diamond Tool and Horseshoe Co.
4620 Grand Ave.
Duluth, Minnesota 55800

Flaghouse, Inc.
80 4th Ave.
New York, New York 10027

Robot Industries, Inc.
7041 Orchard St.
Dearborn, Michigan 48120

Lawn Bowling

Flaghouse, Inc.
80 4th Ave.
New York, New York 10027

Robot Industries, Inc.
7041 Orchard St.
Dearborn, Michigan 48120

Miniature Golf

Animated Display Creations
7301 N. E. Miami Ct.
Miami, Florida 33161

Aura Golf Construction Co.
10923 S. Western Ave.
Chicago, Illinois 60600

Borum Enterprises
909 S. Locust
Centralia, Illinois 62801

Bumpo-Gates Manufacturing Co.
P. O. Box 111
Highway 309
Ozark, Arkansas 72949

Clinton-Kent-Bradley
Box 2
Wayne, New Jersey 07470

Container Development Corp.
5024 Montgomery
Watertown, Wisconsin 53094

Daco Golf Products
4444 W. Belmont
Chicago, Illinois 60600

Davis Felt and Carpet Manufacturing
Co.
Miller St.
Philadelphia, Pennsylvania 19100

Dean Golf Supply Co.
P. O. Box 3285
San Angelo, Texas 76901

Diversified Amusement Co.
Box 202
Clarence Center, New York 14032

Eastern Golf Co.
2537 Boston Rd.
Bronx, New York 10451

Economy Handicrafts, Inc.
Box 210
Little Neck, New York 11363

Holmes Cook Miniature Golf Co.
RD 1
Tamaqua, Pennsylvania 18252

Lomma Enterprises, Inc.
305 Cherry St.
Scranton, Pennsylvania 18500

Robert H. Kraeger Co., Inc.
609 Harper Ave.
Jenkintown, Pennsylvania 19046

Merchants Tire Co.
2710 Washington
St. Louis, Missouri 63100

Miniature Golf Country Clubs, Inc.
29225 S. Woodland
Cleveland, Ohio 44100

Arnold Palmer Putting Courses
14 W. Mulberry
Pleasantville, New Jersey 08232

Putt-Putt Golf Courses of America
P. O. Box 5237
Fayetteville, North Carolina 28301

Rogers Manufacturing Co.
220 N. Mahaffie
Olathe, Kansas 66061

Southern Golf Distributors
3007 Fort Bragg Rd.
Fayetteville, North Carolina 28301

Sporting Goods Discount Co.
3914 Akron-Medina Rd.
Akron, Ohio 44300

Strickly Golf
234 61st St.
Downers Grove, Illinois 60615

Western Golf Sales, Inc.
1831 Colorado Ave.
Santa Monica, California 90406

Wittek Golf Range Supply
3650 Avondale Ave.
Chicago, Illinois 60600

Paddle Tennis

Dayton Racquet Co.
716 Albright Ave.
Arcanum, Ohio 45304

Roller Skating

Chicago Roller Skating Co.
4458 W. Lake St.
Chicago, Illinois 60600

Mitchell Division of Royal Industries
1500 E. Chestnut St.
Santa Ana, California 92700

Ruedell Shoes, Inc.
Industrial Park
Red Wing, Minnesota 55066

Robot Industries, Inc.
7041 Orchard St.
Dearborn, Michigan 48120

Shuffleboard

American Shuffleboard Co.
210 Paterson Plank Rd.
Union City, New Jersey 07087

Bumpo-Gates Manufacturing Co.
P. O. Box 111
Highway 309
Ozark, Arkansas 72949

Dimco-Gray Co.
206 E. 6th St.
Dayton, Ohio 45400

North American Recreation
   Convertibles, Inc.
P. O. Box 668
Westport, Connecticut 06880

Swimming

Gulbenkian Swim, Inc.
87 Greenwich Ave.
Greenwich, Connecticut 06830

Halogen Supply Co.
4653 Lawrence Ave.
Chicago, Illinois 60656

Ocean Pool Supply
17 Stepar Place
Long Island, New York 11102

Seamless Rubber Co.
253 Halloch Ave.
New Haven, Connecticut 06500

Universe Co.
Altadena, California 91001

Swimming Clothing

Kaynell Co.
P. O. Box 230
Little Neck, New York 11363

Table Tennis

All Metal Table Tennis Co.
Box 142
Teaneck, New Jersey 07666

Brinktun, Inc.
Le Center, Minnesota 56057

Marcy Gymnasium Equipment Co.
1736 Standard Ave.
Glendale, California 91200

Midwest Folding Products
1414 S. Western Ave.
Chicago, Illinois 60600

Nissen Corp.
930 27th Ave. S. W.
Cedar Rapids, Iowa 52420

North American Recreation
Convertibles, Inc.
P. O. Box 668
Westport, Connecticut 06880

Pipo Table Tennis Balls
882 Massachusetts Ave.
Indianapolis, Indiana 46200

Sico Aired Bag Co.
8669 Fenwick
Sunland, California 91040

T. F. Twardzik & Co.
600 E. Center St.
Shenandoah, Pennsylvania 17976

Tetherball

J. E. Burke Co.
Fond du Lac, Wisconsin 54135

Game-time, Inc.
Litchfield, Michigan 49252

Everwear Park and Playground
Equipment, Inc.
P. O. Box 291
Oconomowoc, Wisconsin 53066

Jamison, Inc.
19253 S. Vermont Ave.
Torrance, California 90500

Uniforms and Clothing

American Knitwear and Emblem
Manufacturing
Chadwick St.
Plaistow, New Hampshire 03865

Cran Barry, Inc.
P. O. Box 354
2 Lincoln Ave.
Marblehead, Massachusetts 01945

Champion Products
P. O. Box 850
Rochester, New York 14603

Dallas Uniform Cap and Emblem
Manufacturing Co.
Dallas, Texas 75200

Demco
Dana E. Morrison, Jr. Co.
5121 N. Ravenswood Ave.
Chicago, Illinois 60640

Dolphin Sportswear Co.
Shillington, Pennsylvania 19607

Jantzen, Inc.
P. O. Box 3001
Portland, Oregon 97208

E. R. Moore Co.
7230 N. Coldwell Ave.
Niles, Illinois 60648

Rawlings Sporting Goods Co.
2300 Delmar Blvd.
St. Louis, Missouri 63166

Velva Sheen Manufacturing Co.
3860 Virginia Ave.
Cincinnati, Ohio 45227

Volleyball

Ball-Boy Co., Inc.
27 Milburn St.
Bronxville, New York 10708

J. E. Burke Co.
Fond du Lac, Wisconsin 54935

Everwear Park and Playground
    Equipment, Inc.
P. O. Box 291
Oconomowoc, Wisconsin 53066

Game-time, Inc.
903 Anderson Rd.
Litchfield, Michigan 49252

Jamison, Inc.
19253 S. Vermont Ave.
Torrance, California 90500

Nissen Corp.
930 27th Ave. S. W.
Cedar Rapids, Iowa 52420

Sports Award Co.
4351 Milwaukee Ave.
Chicago, Illinois 60600

Superior Net Co.
P. O. Box 237
Highland, Illinois 62249

Victory Sports Products
927 First St.
Menominee, Michigan 49858

West Coast Netting, Inc.
14929 Clark Ave.
City of Industry, California 91744

Wrestling

Atlas Athletic Equipment Co.
2339 Hampton Ave.
St. Louis, Missouri 63139

APPENDIX C

Films, Filmstrips, Loop Films and Records Dealing With Specific Physical Education Activities

THE READER IS directed to the end of each section of the appendix for full addresses of the film and record sources mentioned below the title of each film, filmstrip, loop film and record.

FILMS

Archery

Archery for Girls
10 min.
Coronet Instructional Films

Archery Fundamentals
11 min. color
Bailey Films, Inc.

Art of Archery
12 min. color
Bear Archery

Badminton

Badminton Fundamentals
11 min.
Coronet Instructional Films

Play Badminton with Wong Peng Soon
16mm, sound, 18 min.
Malaysian Mission to the U. N.

Baseball

Batting Fundamentals
11 min.
Coronet Instructional Films

Catching Fundamentals
11 min.
Coronet Instructional Films

Baseball—Batting—Bunting
16mm, sound, 11 min.
Coca-Cola

Baseball—Pitching
16mm, sound, 11 min.
Coca-Cola

Baseball—Tips on Baseball
16mm, sound, 11 min.
Coca-Cola

Infield Play
16mm, sound, 14 min.
Planters Peanuts

Batter Up
16mm, sound, 20 min.
American and National Leagues of
  Professional Baseball Clubs

Batting with Ted Williams
16mm, sound, 29 min.
Association Films, Inc.

Big League Baseball for Little
  Leaguers
16mm, sound, 29 min.
Modern Talking Pictures

Hitting
Sears-Roebuck Co.
The Game of Baseball
Athletic Institute

Throwing (underhand, etc.)
Athletic Institute

Fielding
Athletic Institute

Hitting
Athletic Institute

Catching (positions)
Athletic Institute

Basketball

Basketball for Boys: Fundamentals
11 min.
Bailey Films, Inc.

Bicycle

Magic of the Bicycle
16mm, sound, 27 min.
Association Films, Inc.

Bowling

Let's Go Bowling
16mm, sound, 25 min.
Brunswick Corp.

Bowling Fever
12 min.
Brunswick Corp.

American Bowls
25 min.
Brunswick Corp.

Duck Pin Bowling
26 min.
Brunswick Corp.

Bowling Fundamentals
17 min.
Teaching Films Custodians, Inc.

A Life Time of Bowling
American Association of Health,
　Physical Education and Recreation

How To Improve Your Bowling
Athletic Institute

The Wonderful World of Bowling
Miller Brewing Co.

Bulletin Boards

Bulletin Boards: An Effective Teaching
　Device
16mm, 11 min. color
Bailey Films, Inc.

Dance

American Square Dance
11 min.
Coronet Instructional Films

Football

Catching a Football
16mm, sound, 11 min.
Coca-Cola

Gymnastics

Trampoline Fundamentals
11 min.
Bailey Films, Inc.

Simple Stunts
10 min.
Coronet Instructional Films

Headsprings in the Gym
9 min.
Encyclopedia Britannica Educational
　Films, Inc.

Gymnastics for Girls
30 min. color
Association Films, Inc.

Gymnastics in Japan
16mm, sound, 29 min.
Consulate General of Japan

Ice Hockey

Hot Ice
11 min.
National Film Board of Canada

Ice Skating

Figure Skating
16mm, sound, 25 min.
Consulate General of Canada

Lacrosse

Lacrosse
16mm, sound, 14 min.
Consulate General of Canada

Learning Lacrosse-Part I and II
Consulate General of Canada

Movement Education

Basic Movement Education in England
19 min.
University of Michigan

Rhythmic Ball Exercises
16mm, sound, 13 min.
Consulate General of Finland

Physical Education

Fitness Skills for Children: Move Better
10 min.
McGraw-Hill Book Co.

Fitness Skills for Children: Play Better
10 min.
McGraw-Hill Book Co.

Lever to Learning
16mm, sound, color, 20 min.
Stuart Finley, Inc.

Planning Creative Play Equipment for
   Young Children
16 min. color
International Film Bureau

Physical and Motor Development of
   Children
20 min.
Central Michigan University

Physical Education for Blind Children
16mm, sound, color, 20 min.
Charles Buell

Up and Over
16mm, sound, color, 25 min.
Bradley Wright Films

Safety

Let's Play Safe
10 min.
Wayne County Library

Playground Safety
11 min.
Coronet Instructional Films

Primary Safety: On the school
   Playground
11 min.
Coronet Instructional Films

Safety on the Playground (2nd. ed.)
Encyclopedia Britannica
   Educational Films, Inc.

Softball

Softball for Boys
10 min.
Coronet Instructional Films

Softball Fundamentals for Elementary
   Schools
11 min.
Bailey Films, Inc.

Swimming

Beginning Swimming
10 min.
Coronet Instructional Films

It's Fun to Swim
16mm, sound, 11½ min.
American Red Cross

Learning How To Swim
16mm, sound, 28 min.
American Red Cross and
   United World Films, Inc.

Swimming and Safety Drownproofing
16mm, sound, 10 min.
Kiekhoefer Corp.

Swimming for a Congenital
   Quad Amputee
16mm. silent, black and white, 10 min.
University of Texas

Swimming for Survival
11 min.
United World Films, Inc.

Water Safety
11 min.
Young America Films, Inc.

Tennis

Fundamentals of Tennis
21 min.
Young America Films, Inc.

Tennis Everyone
16mm, sound, 14½ min.
Coca-Cola Co.

Track and Field

Fundamentals of Track and Field
26 min.
Encyclopedia Britannica Educational
    Films

Track
30 min.
University of Michigan

Track-Basic Jumping Techniques
16mm, sound, 11 min.
Coca-Cola Co.

Volleyball

Fundamentals of Volleyball
10 min.
All American Productions

Wrestling

Takedowns and Counters (Part I,
    Wrestling Fundamentals and
    Techniques)
12 min.
University of Michigan

Addresses of Film Sources

All American Productions
P. O. Box 801
Riverside, California 92502

American and National Leagues of
    Professional Baseball Clubs
200 E. Michigan Ave.
Chicago, Illinois 60600

American Association of Health,
    Physical Education and Recreation
1201 16th Street, S. W.
Washington, D. C. 20024

American Red Cross
Contact your local chapter
Association Films, Inc.
347 Madison Ave.
New York, New York 10017

Athletic Institute
805 Merchandise Mart
Chicago, Illinois 60654

Bailey Films, Inc.
6509 De Longpre Ave.
Hollywood, California 90028

Bear Archery
Grayling, Michigan 49738

Bradley Wright Films
309 Duane Ave.
San Gabriel, California 91755

Brunswick Corp.
69 W. Washington St.
Chicago, Illinois 60600

Charles Buell
4244 Heather Ave.
Long Beach, California 90808

Central Michigan University
Audio-Visual Department
Materials Section
Mount Pleasant, Michigan 48858

Coca-Cola Co.
Contact local bottler

Coronet Instructional Films
65 E. Waters St.
Chicago, Illinois 60600

Consulate General of Canada
1920 First Federal Building
Detroit, Michigan 48226

Consulate General of Finland
200 E. 42nd St.
New York, New York 10027

Consulate General of Japan
600 Madison Ave.
New York, New York 10017

Encyclopaedia Britannica
Educational Films, Inc.
P. O. Box 358
Wilmette, Illinois 60600

International Film Bureau
332 S. Michigan Ave.
Chicago, Illinois 60600

Kiekhoefer Corp.
1939 Pioneer Rd.
Fond du Lac, Wisconsin 54935

Malaysian Mission to the
    United Nations
New York, New York 10027

McGraw-Hill Book Co.
330 W. 42nd St.
New York, New York 10018

Miller Brewing Co.
4000 West St.
Milwaukee, Wisconsin 53200

Modern Talking Pictures
1212 Avenue of the Americas
New York, New York 10027

National Film Board of Canada
Sterling Movies, Inc.
43 W. 6th St.
New York, New York 10027

Planters Peanuts
Arthur Mokin Productions
17 W. 60th St.
New York, New York 10027

Sears-Roebuck Co.
925 S. Haman Ave.
Chicago, Illinois 60600

Stuart Finley, Inc.
3428 Mansfield Rd.
Falls Church, Virginia 22041

Teaching Films Custodians, Inc.
25 W. 43rd St.
New York, New York 10016

United World Film, Inc.
1445 Park Ave.
New York, New York 10003

University of Michigan
Audio-Visual Center
Ann Arbor, Michigan 48104

University of Texas
Instructional Media Center
University Station
Austin, Texas 78712

Wayne County Library
Audio-Visual Department
33030 Van Born Rd.
Wayne, Michigan 48184

Young America Films, Inc.
18 E. 41st St.
New York, New York 10017

FILMSTRIPS

Archery

Shooting
Athletic Institute

Aiming
Athletic Institute

Archery Rules
Athletic Institute

Baseball

Throwing
Athletic Institute

Hitting
Athletic Institute

Catching
Athletic Institute

Basketball

Passing
Athletic Institute

Dribbling
Athletic Institute

Shooting
Athletic Institute

Bicycling

Riding Fundamentals
Athletic Institute

Bowling

Learning How to Bowl
American Association of Health,
 Physical Education and Recreation

Aiming
Athletic Institute

Delivery
Athletic Institute

Scoring
Athletic Institute

Bulletin Boards

Bulletin Boards at Work
Wayne State University

Games

Running
Teacher Products

Stopping and Turning
Athletic Institute

Tagging-No Goal
Athletic Institute

Evading and Dodging
Athletic Institute

Jumping
Teacher Products

Golf

Putting
Athletic Institute

Field Hockey

The Sport
Athletic Institute

Fishing

Hook-and-Line Fundamentals
Athletic Institute

Let's Go Fishing
Athletic Institute

Gymnastics

Balance Beam
Athletic Institute

Side Horse Vaulting
Athletic Institute

Free Exercise and Vaulting (Girls)
Athletic Institute

Apparatus Fun
BFA Educational Media

Physical Education

Fitness-Exercises and Stunts
Eastern Michigan University

Fitness-Rhythmical Activities
Eastern Michigan University

Physical Education-Primary
Audio-Visual Education

Physical Education
Audio-Visual Education

Fitness: Team Games
Society for Visual Education

Stunts and Creative Activities
Teacher Products

Safety

School Safety
Nasco Instructional Materials

Play Safety
Nasco Instructional Materials

Soccer

The Game
Athletic Institute

Controlling the Ball
Athletic Institute

Softball

Fielding
Athletic Institute

Swimming

Getting Used to the Water
Athletic Institute

Learning to Swim
Athletic Institute

Learn to Swim
BFA Educational Media

The Elementary Back Stroke
Athletic Institute

Table Tennis

The Fundamentals
Athletic Institute

Tennis

Getting Ready to Play
Athletic Institute

The Game
Athletic Institute

Track and Field

(Elementary Level)
Track Events
Athletic Institute

Field Events
Athletic Institute

Tumbling

Individual Balancing
Athletic Institute

Singles Tumbling
Athletic Institute

Trampoline

Introduction to Trampolining
Athletic Institute

Wrestling

Introduction to Wrestling
Athletic Institute

Wrestling Fundamentals
Kimbo Educational

Addresses of Filmstrip Sources

American Association of Health,
Physical Education and Recreation
1210 16th St., S. W.
Washington, D. C. 20024

Association Instructional Materials
A Division of Association Films, Inc.
600 Madison Ave.
New York, New York 10022

Audio Visual Education
15920 Grand River
Detroit, Michigan 48227

Bailey-Film Associates
11559 Santa Monica Blvd.
Los Angeles, California 90025

BFA Educational Media
2211 Michigan Ave.
Santa Monica, California 90404

Eastern Michigan University
Audio-Visual Department
Materials Section
Ypsilanti, Michigan 48197

Kimbo Educational
P. O. Box 246
Deal, New Jersey 07723

Nasco Instructional Materials
Fort Atkinson, Wisconsin 53538

Society for Visual Education
1345 Diversey Parkway
Chicago, Illinois 60614

Teacher Products
2304 E. Johnson
Jonesboro, Arkansas 72401

Wayne State University
Audio-Visual Department
Wayne, Michigan 48222

LOOP FILMS

Archery

Use of Bow
Harold C. Amrosch

Badminton

Grip and Cocking
Athletic Institute

High Deep Serve
Athletic Institute

Low Short Serve
Athletic Institute

Drive Shot
Athletic Institute

Baseball

Hitting-Stance and Swing
Athletic Institute

Hitting-Netting the Pitches
Athletic Institute

Fielding the Ground Ball
Athletic Institute

Basketball

Basketball Fundamentals
16mm
Wolverine Sports Supply

Passing and Catching
BFA Educational Media

Baseball Pass
BFA Educational Media

Set Shot
BFA Educational Media

Bounce Pass
Potter's Photographic Applications Co.

Lay-up-shot with One Step
Charles Cahill and Associates, Inc.

Dribbling
Charles Cahill and Associates, Inc.

Bowling

One Step Delivery
Ealing Film-Loops

Gymnastics

Tumbling 1
Ealing Film-Loops

Forward Roll-Backward Roll
Athletic Institute

Back Extension
Athletic Institute

Cartwheel
Athletic Institute

Squat Headbalance-Squat Handbalance
Athletic Institute

Women's Gymnastics
Association Instructional Materials

Parallel Bars

Parallel Bars 1
Ealing Film-Loops

Still Rings

Basic Movements
Athletic Institute

Rings 1
Ealing Film-Loops

Trampoline

Trampoline 1
Ealing Film-Loops

Beginning Routine
Athletic Institute

Basic Bounces
Athletic Institute

Basic Trampoline
Wolverine Sports Supply

Swivel Hips-Turntable
Athletic Institute

Movement Education

Moving in Many Directions
Ealing Film-Loops

Moving at Different Levels
Ealing Film-Loops

Shapes
Ealing Film-Loops

Supports
Ealing Film-Loops

Movement Education With Apparatus

Yarn Balls, Hoops, Ropes and Wands
Ealing Film-Loops

Throwing and Catching
Ealing Film-Loops

Soccer

Kicking
Athletic Institute

Trapping-Ground Balls
Athletic Institute

Softball

Batting
BFA Educational Media

Throwing
Charles Cahill and Associates, Inc.

Catching (fly ball)
Charles Cahill and Associates, Inc.

Swimming

Teaching Beginners
Macmillan & Co., Ltd.

Men's Swimming
Wolverine Sports Supply

Tennis

Tennis
Association Instruction Materials

Girl's Tennis
Wolverine Sports Supply

Addresses for Loop Film Sources

Harold C. Amrosch
P. O. Box 3
Rancho Mirage, California 92270

Association Instructional Materials
A Division of Association Films, Inc.
600 Madison Ave.
New York, New York 10022

Athletic Institute
805 Merchandise Mart
Chicago, Illinois 60654

BFA Educational Media
2211 Michigan Ave.
Santa Monica, California 90404

Charles Cahill and Associates, Inc.
P. O. Box 3220
Hollywood, California 90028

Ealing Film-Loops
Holt, Rinehart and Winston, Inc.,

Publishers
383 Madison Ave.
New York, New York 10017

MacMillan & Co., Ltd.
Write to: Audio-Visual Systems
27 Hass Rd.
Toronto, Canada

Potter's Photographic Applications Co.
160 Herricks Rd.
Mineola, New York 10017

Wolverine Sports Supply
745 State Circle
Ann Arbor, Michigan 48104

Records

FOLK DANCE

Popular and Folk Music for Special
Education
Hoctor Dance Records, Inc.

Beginning Modern American Folk
  Dances
33⅓ rpm
Educational Record Sales

World of Fun for Folk Dances
  and Games
33⅓ rpm
Educational Activities, Inc.

Mexican Folk Dances
78 rpm
Educational Record Sales

International Folk Dances
33⅓ rpm
Educational Activities, Inc.

Canadian Folk Dances
33⅓ rpm
Educational Record Sales

African Heritage Dances
33⅓ rpm
Educational Activities, Inc.

Dances Without Partners
33⅓ rpm
Educational Record Sales

Games

Lummi Sticks
33⅓ rpm, Album
Educational Activities, Inc.

Ribbon Dance
33⅓ rpm, Album
Educational Activities, Inc.

Bamboo Hop
33⅓ rpm, Album
Educational Activities, Inc.

POI-POI
33⅓ rpm, Album
Educational Activities, Inc.

Gymnastics

Stunts and Tumbling for Elementary
  School Children
33⅓ rpm
Educational Activities, Inc.

Rhythmic Gymnastics Using Hand
  Apparatus
Kimbo Educational

Ball Gymnastics
33⅓ rpm
Kimbo Educational

Movement Education

Creative Music for Exceptional
  Children
33⅓ rpm, Album
Kimbo Educational

Music for Movement Exploration
33⅓ rpm, Album
Kimbo Educational

Rhythms and Songs for Exceptional
  Children
33⅓ rpm, Album
Kimbo Educational

Multi-Purpose Singing Games
Educational Activities, Inc.

Fundamental Rhythms
33⅓ rpm
Educational Activities, Inc.

Primary Musical Games
78 rpm
Educational Activities, Inc.

Children's Dance Time
Nasco Instructional Materials

Action and Imitative
Nasco Instructional Materials

Rhythmic Parachute Play
33⅓ rpm
Educational Activities, Inc.

Creative Rhythms
School Specialty Supply, Inc.

Dance, Sing and Listen
Newman Educational Records

Words and Movement about Myself
  and Musical Games
Nasco Instructional Materials

Jumpnastics
Educational Activities, Inc.

Physical Education

Songs and Games of Physical Fitness
33⅓ rpm
Educational Record Sales

Physical Fitness and Self-Expression
  Songs
Educational Record Sales

Skip Rope Games
33⅓ rpm
Educational Record Sales

27 Rhythms for Physical Fitness
Educational Record Sales

15 for Physical Fitness
(Exceptional Children)
Lyons Band Instrument Co.

Fitness Fun for Everyone
(Exceptional Children)
Lyons Band Instrument Co.

Physical Fitness for the Younger Set
(Exceptional Children)
Lyons Band Instrument Co.

And The Beat Goes On For Physical
  Education
Lyons Band Instrument Co.

Physical Education for Primary Grades
School Specialty Supply, Inc.

Developmental Exercises for
  Elementary Grades
Hoctor Dance Records, Inc.
Activity Songs

Newman Educational Records
Music Participation Stories
Audio Visual Education

Get Fit While You Sit
Educational Activities, Inc.

Square Dancing

Basic Square Dance Music
Educational Activities, Inc.

Square Dancing Made Easy
Educational Record Sales

Singing Square Dances
Educational Record Sales

Square Dancing
School Specialty Supply, Inc.

Swimming

Swimming Skills and Dry Land Drills
Lyons Band Instrument Co.

Addresses for Record Sources

Audio Visual Education
15920 Grand River
Detroit, Michigan 48227

Educational Activities, Inc.
P. O. Box 392
Freeport, New York 11520

Educational Record Sales
157 Chambers St.
New York, New York 10007

Hoctor Dance Records, Inc.
Waldwick, New Jersey 07463

Kimbo Educational
P. O. Box 246
Deal, New Jersey 07723

Lyons Band Instrument Co.
688 Industrial Dr.
Elmhurst, Illinois 60126

Nasco Instructional Materials
Fort Atkinson, Wisconsin 53538

Newman Educational Records
2023 Eastern Ave.
Grand Rapids, Michigan 49507

RCA Records
Educational Department
1133 Avenue of the Americas
New York, New York 10036

School Specialty Supply, Inc.
P. O. Box 1327
212-218 Santa Fe
Salina, Kansas 67401

Film Distributors for Specific Physical Education Activities

APPENDIX D CONTAINS additional film sources for physical educational activities that do not appear in Appendix C.

Baseball

Ethan Allen
Films on Sports
402A Yale Station
New Haven, Connecticut 06500

Sears-Roebuck Co.
925 S. Haman Ave.
Chicago, Illinois 60600

Basketball

Association Films, Inc.
Executive Offices
600 Madison Ave.
New York, New York 10022

Films may be obtained from the following Association Films addresses:

2221 Faulkner Rd. N. E.
Atlanta, Georgia 30324

1621 Dragon St.
Dallas, Texas 75207

25358 Cypress Ave.
Hayward, California 94544

561 Hillgrove Ave.
LaGrange, Illinois 60525

490 King St.
Littleton, Massachusetts 01460

2221 S. Olive St.
Los Angeles, California 90007

324 Delaware Ave.
Oakmont, Pennsylvania 15139

600 Grand Ave.
Ridgefield, New Jersey 07657

Coca-Cola Co.
Contact local bottler of Coca-Cola

Phillips Petroleum Co.
Film Library
310 W. 5th St.
Bartlesville, Oklahoma 74003

Fishing

Arkansas Publicity and Parks
  Commission
149 State Capitol Building
Little Rock, Arkansas 72201

General Motors Co.
Public Relations Staff
Film Library
General Motors Building
Detroit, Michigan 48202

Kiekhaefer Corp.
Film Library
1939 Pioneer Rd.
Fond du Lac, Wisconsin 54935

Motion Picture Film Library
424 Main St.
Buffalo, New York 14202

Films may be obtained from the following Motion Picture Film Library addresses:

150 W. Adams St.
Chicago, Illinois 60603

131 W. Lafayette Blvd.
Detroit, Michigan 48226

108 E. Kearsly St.
Flint, Michigan 48502

510 E. 6th St.
Los Angeles, California 90014

527 Marquette Ave.
Minneapolis, Minnesota 55402

630 5th Ave.
New York, New York 10020

314 N. Broadway
St. Louis, Missouri 63102

210 Post St.
San Francisco, California 94108

514 Vance Building
Seattle, Washington 98101

United Aircraft Corp.
Public Relations Department
East Hartford, Connecticut 06108

Folk Dance

Information Service of India
Film Section
3 E. 64th St.
New York, New York 10021
(Contact above address for state location serving your area)

Allstate Insurance Co.
Public Relations Director
Allstate Plaza
Northbrook, Illinois 60062

Planters Peanuts
Arthur Mokin Productions
17 W. 16th St.
New York, New York 10023

Golf

Florida Development Commission
Film Library
Collins Building
Tallahassee, Florida 32304

Reynolds Metals Co.
Motion Picture Department
P. O. Box 2346
Richmond, Virginia 23218

Ice Hockey

Consulate General of Canada
500 Boylston St.
Boston, Massachusetts 02116

Quebec Government House
The Film Office
17 W. 50th St.
New York, New York 10020

Softball

Amateur Softball Association
1351 Skirvin Tower
Oklahoma City, Oklahoma 73102

Square Dancing

World of Fun Records
1661 Northwest Highway
Park Ridge, Illinois 60068

APPENDIX E

Audiovisual Aid Suppliers

THE FOLLOWING COMPANIES or manufacturers are suppliers of audiovisual aid materials that can be used in the adapted physical education program. They are suppliers of such aids as films, film-strips, bulletin board materials, records or projection equipment.

Abington Press
201 8th Ave.
Nashville, Tennessee 37200
Records

All American Products
P. O. Box 91
Greely, Colorado 80632
16mm motion picture films

American Association of Health,
  Physical Education and Recreation
1201 16th St., N. W.
Washington, D. C. 20005
Slide films and teaching manual

American Dental Association
222 E. Superior St.
Chicago, Illinois 60611
Safety Films

American Film Registry
831 Wabash Ave.
Chicago, Illinois 60605

American Instructional Materials, Inc.
Box 22748
Denton, Texas 76240
Loop films

American National Red Cross
17th and D Streets, N. W.
Washington, D. C. 20006
Safety films

Associated Films, Inc.
347 Madison Ave.
New York, New York 10017

Associated Films
561 Hilgrove
La Grange, Illinois 60525

Athletic Institute
805 Merchandise Mart
Chicago, Illinois 60600
35 mm film strips
8mm loop films
teaching manuals

Audio-Film Center/Ideal Pictures
34 McQuesten Parkway S.
Mount Vernon, New York 10550

Avis Films, Inc.
904 E. Palm Ave.
Burbank, California 91501
Safety films

Bailey Films, Inc.
6509 De Longpre Ave.
Hollywood, California 90028

Bell and Howell
7100 McCormick
Chicago, Illinois 60645
Projectors

Bowman
622 Rodier Dr.
Glendale, California 91200

Brewster Corp.
50 River St.
Old Saybrook, Connecticut 06475

Canyon Films, Inc.
834 N. 7th St.
Phoenix, Arizona 85007

198

Card-Key Systems, Inc.
901 S. San Fernando Rd.
Burbank, California 91503

Champions on Films
3666 S. State St.
Ann Arbor, Michigan 48014
16mm loop films
35mm film strips

Clem Williams Films
2240 Noblestown Rd.
Pittsburgh, Pennsylvania 15205

Contemporary Films, Inc.
267 W. 25th St.
New York, New York 10001

Coronet Instructional Films
65 E. South Water St.
Chicago, Illinois 60601

Dance Records
1438 Springvale Ave.
McLean Virginia 22101

Demco Educational Corp.
Box 1488
Madison, Wisconsin 53701

Ealing Films
2225 Massachusetts Ave.
Cambridge, Massachusetts 02138

Ebsco Industries, Inc.
1st Avenue North at 13th St.
Birmingham, Alabama 35201

East House Enterprise, Inc.
300 Park Avenue S.
New York, New York 10027
Films

Educational Activities, Inc.
1937 Grand Ave.
Baldwin, New York 11510
Films

Educational Screen, Inc.
64 E. Lake St.
Chicago, Illinois 60601

Educational Service Program
557 Columbus Ave.
New Haven, Connecticut 06500

Encyclopaedia Britannica Films, Inc.
1150 Wilmette Ave.
Wilmette, Illinois 60091

Folkraft
1159 Broad St.
Newark, New Jersey 07114

Films, Inc.
1144 Wilmette Ave.
Wilmette, Illinois 60091

Ideal Pictures
1010 Church St.
Evanston, Illinois 60201

Institutional Cinema Service, Inc.
29 E. 10th St.
New York, New York 10003

Kelly's Industrial Photography, Inc.
324 W. Pico Blvd.
Los Angeles, California 90003

Levey's Film and Projection Service
1648 Pullman Ave.
Cincinnati, Ohio 45200

Listening Library
1 Park Ave.
Old Greenwich, Connecticut 06870
Records

McGraw Hill Book Co.
330 W. 42nd St.
New York, New York 10036

Metropolitan Life Insurance Co.
1 Madison Ave.
New York, New York 10027
Films

Michigan Department of Mental
   Health
Education Department
Lewis Cass Building
Lansing, Michigan 48905
Films

Mike Roberts Color Products
2023 8th St.
Berkeley, California 94710
Films

Miller Brewing Co.
4000 West St.
Milwaukee, Wisconsin 53200

Modern Talking Pictures
4754 Woodward Ave.
Detroit, Michigan 48207
16mm films

Nasco Instructional Materials
919 Jonesville Ave.
Fort Atkinson, Wisconsin 53538
Films

National Safety Council
422 N. Michigan Ave.
Chicago, Illinois 60611
Films

National Song Slide, Inc.
42 W. 48th St.
New York, New York 10036

Northern Films
Box 98 Main Office Station
Seattle, Washington 98100

Perma-Power Co.
5740 N. Tripp Ave.
Chicago, Illinois 60646
Films

Record Center
2581 Piedmont Rd., N. E.
Atlanta, Georgia 30324

Rheem Califone Corp.
5922 Bowercraft
Los Angeles, California 90016

Rhythms Production Records
Whitney Biuilding
Box 34485
Los Angeles, California 90003

Russell Records, Inc.
P. O. Box 3318
Ventura, California 93803

Society for Visual Education, Inc.
1345 Diversey Parkway
Chicago, Illinois 60614

Solocast Co.
999 Bedford St.
Stamford, Connecticut 06906

Solar
4247 S. Kedzie Ave.
Chicago, Illinois 60632

Sound Associates, Inc.
318 W. 48th St.
New York, New York 10027

Sound Equipment
331 W. 51st St.
New York, New York 10027

Sterling Movies, Inc.
6 E. 39th St.
New York, New York 10027

Strong Electronic Corp.
P. O. Box 1003
Toledo, Ohio 43601

Theatre Production Service
52 W. 46th St.
New York, New York 10027

Tru-Scale, Inc.
Shoco Division
1123 N. Mosly
Wichita, Kansas 67230

Tyman Films, Inc.
329 Salem Ave.
Dayton, Ohio 45401

Universal Education and Visual Arts
221 Park Ave. S.
New York, New York 10027

Visual Industrial Products, Inc.
P. O. Box 113
Oakmont, Pennsyvania 15139

Windsor Record Co.
5530 Rosemead Blvd.
Temple City, California 91780

Films Dealing with Mental and Physical Handicaps

Blind and Partially Sighted

Visually Handicapped Child:
  The Blind
29 min.
Jewish Community Council of
  Metropolitan Detroit
163 Madison Ave.
Detroit, Michigan 48232

Visually Handicapped Child:
  Partially Sighted
29 min.
Jewish Community Council of
  Metropolitan Detroit
163 Madison Ave.
Detroit, Michigan 48232

Cardiac

Common Heart Disorders and
  Their Causes
17 min.
McGraw-Hill Book Co.
330 W. 42nd St.
New York, New York 10036

Rheumatic Fever
30 min.
University of Michigan
Ann Arbor, Micihgan 48108

Valiant Heart
30 min.
American Heart Association
44 E. 23rd St.
New York, New York 10027

We See Them Through
  (Rheumatic Fever)
20 min.

Michigan Department of Health,
  Audio-Visual
Education Service
3500 Logan St.
Lansing, Michigan 48900

Cerebral Palsy

Camping Makes Life Worth Living
16mm, sound, 15 min.

United Cerebral Palsy
  Associations, Inc.
66 E. 34th St.
New York, New York 10036

Cerebral Palsied Child
29 min.
Jewish Community Council of
  Metropolitan Detroit
163 Madison Ave.
Detroit, Michigan 48232

These Are Our Children
16mm, sound, 15 min.
United Cerebral Palsy
  Associations, Inc.
66 E. 34th St.
New York, New York 10036

What Is Cerebral Palsy?
16mm, sound, 17½ min.
United Cerebral Palsy
  Associations, Inc.
66 E. 34th St.
New York, New York 10036

Deaf

Auditorially Handicapped Child:
  The Deaf

29 min.
Jewish Community Council of
  Metropolitan Detroit
163 Madison Ave.
Detroit, Michigan 48232

Epilepsy

Epileptic Child
28 min.
Jewish Community Council of
  Metropolitan Detroit
163 Madison Ave.
Detroit, Michigan 48232

Epileptic Seizure Patterns
25 min.
Jewish Community Council of
  Metropolitan Detroit
163 Madison Ave.
Detroit, Michigan 48232

Grand Mal Epilepsy
16 mm, color, sound, 30 min.
Ideal Pictures Offices
417 N. State St.
Chicago, Illinois 60600

Exceptional Children

Cast No Shadow
16mm, sound, color, 27 min.
Professional Arts, Inc.
Universal City, California 91608

Chronic Disorders
29 min.
Jewish Community Council of
  Metropolitan Detroit
163 Madison Ave.
Detroit, Michigan 48232

Hard-of-Hearing

Pay Attention: Problems
  of Hard-of-Hearing Children
31 min.
New York University
New York, New York 10036

Mentally Retarded

Anyone Can
16mm, sound, color, 27 min.
Bradley Wright Films
309 N. Duane Ave.
San Gabriel, California 91773

Below Average
30 min.
Wayne State University
Audio-Visual Utilization Center
5454 Cass Ave.
Detroit, Michigan 48232

Beyond The Shadows
26 min.
Michigan Department of Health
Audio-Visual Education Service
3500 N. Logan St.
Lansing, Michigan 48911

Bob and His Friends on the
  Playground
5 min.
Educational Materials Distributors
Weslaco, Texas 78956
Taken from Education and Welfare,
  Social and Rehabilitation Service

Children Limited
30 min.
Muskegon County Board of Education
Instructional Services Department
Muskegon, Michigan 49440

Class for Tommy
20 min.
Central Michigan University
Bureau of Audio-Visual Aids
Mount Pleasant, Michigan 48858

Introducing the Mentally Retarded
22 min.
Michigan Department of Health
Audio-Visual Education Services
3500 N. Logan St.
Lansing, Michigan 48911

Mentally Handicapped: Educable
29 min.
Jewish Community Council of
  Metropolitan Detroit
163 Madison Ave.
Detroit, Michigan 48232

Mentally Retarded: Trainable
29 min.
Jewish Community Council of
  Metropolitan Detroit
163 Madison Ave.
Detroit, Michigan 48232

Patterns
16 mm, sound, color, 17 min.
Guy Owen, Title III Physical
  Education Research Grant
P. O. Box 1269
Austin, Texas 78702

Michael: A Mongoloid Child
14 min.
Central Michigan University
Bureau of Audio-Visual Aids
Mount Pleasant, Michigan 48858

Report on Down's Syndrome
  (Mongolism)
14 min.
Michigan Department of Health
Audio-Visual Educational Service
3500 N. Logan St.
Lansing, Michigan 48911

Physically Handicapped

Common Threads
20 min.
University of Michigan
Audio-Visual Educational Center
Frieze Building
720 E. Huron St.
Ann Arbor, Michigan

Crippled Child
29 min.
Jewish Community Council of
  Metropolitan Detroit
163 Madison Ave.
Detroit, Michigan 48232

Additional Film Sources Dealing With Mental And Physical Handicaps

American Heart Association
44 E. 23rd St.
New York, New York 10027

Associations of American Medical
  Colleges
2530 Ridge Ave.
Evanston, Illinois 60200

Ayerst Laboratories
22 E. 40th St.
New York, New York 10027

Coronet Instructional Films
65 E. South Water St.
Chicago, Illinois 60600

Encyclopaedia Britannica
  Educational Films
1150 Wilmette Ave.
Wilmette, Illinois 60091

Epilepsy Information Center
73 Tremont St.
Boston, Massachusetts 02100

Guidance Information Center
Academy Ave.
Saxtons River, Vermont 05154

The March of Dimes National
  Foundation
800 Second Ave.
New York, New York 10027

McGraw-Hill Book Co.
330 W. 42nd St.
New York, New York 10036

National Epilepsy League
203 N. Wabash Ave.
Chicago, Illinois 60600

Sterling Movies
Booking Department
390 W. Jackson St.
Chicago, Illinois 60600

United Epilepsy Association
111 W. 57th St.
New York, New York 10027

INDEX

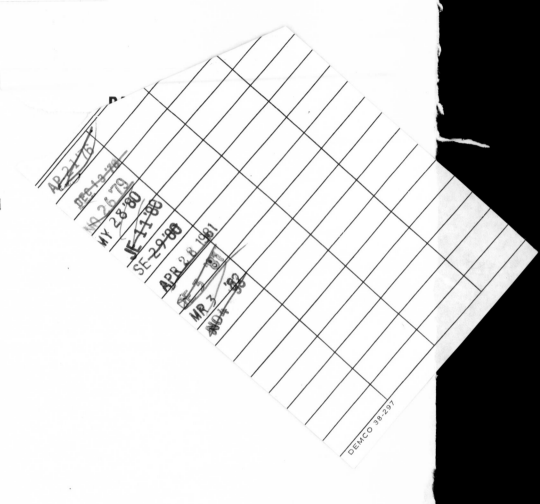

DEMCO 38-297